Catholic Beliefs
From A to Z

Catholic Beliefs
From A to Z

Rev. Alfred McBride, O.Praem.

CHARIS

SERVANT PUBLICATIONS
ANN ARBOR, MICHIGAN

Charis Books is an imprint of Servant Publications especially designed to serve Roman Catholics.

All Scripture quotations, unless indicated, are taken from the HOLY BIBLE, NEW INTERNA-
TIONAL VERSION® 1973, 1978, 1984 by International Bible Society. Used by permission of
Zondervan Publishing House. All rights reserved. Verses marked NAB are taken from the New
American Bible. The Old Testament of the New American Bible © 1970 by the Confraternity of
Christian Doctrine (CCD), Washington, D.C. (Books 1 Samuel to 2 Maccabees ©1969; Revised
New Testament of the New American Bible ©1986 CCD; Revised Psalms of the New American
Bible ©1991 CCD. All rights reserved.

Excerpts from the English translation of the *Catechism of the Catholic Church* for use in the
United States of America. © 1994, United States Catholic Conference, Inc.—Libreria Editrice
Vaticana. Used with Permission.

Servant Publications
P.O. Box 8617
Ann Arbor, MI 48107

Cover design by Paz Design Group

01 02 03 04 10 9 8 7 6 5 4 3 2 1

Printed in the United States of America
ISBN 1-56955-174-X

Library of Congress Cataloging-in-Publication Data

McBride, Alfred
    Catholic beliefs from A to Z / Alfred McBride.
        p. cm.
    Includes index.
    ISBN 1-56955-174-X (alk. paper)
    1. Catholic Church—Dictionaries. I. Title.

BX841 .M37 2001
230'.2—dc21

2001017362

Introduction

My words fly up, my thoughts remain below:
Words without thoughts never to heaven go.

Hamlet III, iii, 97

Perhaps St. John the evangelist would make a good patron for this book because he opens his Gospel with a description of Jesus Christ as the Word. This is a book about words that Catholics use to speak and write about their faith. Catholic beliefs are expressed in words that ultimately flow from the Word made flesh. With his customary poetic sense, St. John of the Cross alludes to this when he writes: "In giving us his Son, his only Word ... he spoke everything to us at once in this sole word—and he has no more to say."[1]

The power and value of words have been celebrated often, but seldom with the eloquence dramatized in a brief scene from Robert Bolt's play *A Man for All Seasons,* set in Reformation England. Parliament has passed an act requiring people to take an oath recognizing Henry VIII's invalid marriage to Anne Boleyn. St. Thomas More, who opposed the king's marriage, wonders as he talks with his son-in-law, William Roper, whether the words of the oath are composed in such a way that he might take it without compromising his conscience.

MORE: (*Very still.*) What is the oath?

ROPER: (*Puzzled.*) It's about the marriage, sir.

MORE: But what is the wording?

ROPER: We don't need to know ... the wording—we know what it will mean!

MORE: It will mean what the words say! An oath is *made* of words. It may be possible to take it.[2]

---

[1] St. John of the Cross, The Ascent of Mount Carmel, 2, 22,3, in The Collected Works of St. John of the Cross, trans. Kieran Kavanaugh, O.C.D., and Otilio Rodriguez, O.C.D. (Washington, D.C.: ICS Publications, 1979), 179.

[2] Robert Bolt, *A Man for All Seasons: A Play in Two Acts* (New York: Vintage Books, 1960), 72.

More is not equivocating. He is showing respect for the subtlety of words that can allow for retaining one's integrity and yet reasonably satisfy the dangerous demands of authority. As it turned out, the words left no opening for More. He could not take the oath. The crown sent him to the Tower of London and finally to death for his fidelity to Catholic beliefs as taught by Christ and the Church.

Beliefs Are More Than Mere Words

The purpose of Catholic beliefs is to open us to the power of the Holy Spirit, who brings us Christ's salvation from sin and the gift of divine life. Beliefs are never meant to be mere words. They point to thoughts, convictions, and the experience of God's active presence in the world and in the center of the human soul. Faith confronts the deepest of all human questions—the origin and destiny of each human being.

Catholic beliefs cover a number of topics ranging from the creed, sacraments, moral teachings, prayer, and lives of saints to religious customs arising from cultural inclinations. Theologically, they start with the Trinity, focus on Christ, rest in the Church, appear in the sacraments, and are witnessed to in the lives of believers. God's revelation begins it all. Faith in God is the authentic response. Spirit-guided Church history probes and unfolds revelation's meaning and application.

I address this book to anyone who is seeking truth and faith and God. It seems to me that behind this search is the desire to be truly happy. This happiness arises from interior joy provided by the Spirit, far more than from exterior pleasure momentarily yielded by material things. The offer of happiness comes from God and the Church. Catholic beliefs have always been rooted in this conviction.

I also think the book will interest people who are curious about Catholicism as well as cradle Catholics who have questions about various issues of faith. Much has been written about religious literacy in recent years, whether mastery of doctrine or of sacred Scripture. Numerous efforts have been mounted to minister to this need.

A text such as this one is a piece of the puzzle, an organized list of terms that constitute the major vocabulary of an informed Catholic. The alphabetical format has the convenience of putting words and ideas into a predictable sequence.

While this approach lays aside a coherence that would come from an orderly exposition of doctrine, it does provide cross-references that tie strains of thought together.

In exploring ways to define a given word, I relied on the *Catechism of the Catholic Church,* Scripture, liturgical texts, papal pronouncements, theological writings, and spiritual authors. Generally, I sought the shortest way to interpret a word but I often supplied various shades of meaning that provide the richer texture the word deserves.

The Uniqueness of Faith Words

The English language both denotes and connotes words. *Denotation* refers to a definition as close as one can reasonably state. *Connotation* refers to varieties of meaning that flow from the basic understanding.

Religious words are no different in this sense. They come out of the same human mouths from which all terms proceed. In fact, it is the humanity of words that makes them both captivating and sometimes disconcerting, since they insist on being just as surprising and volatile as their human authors.

Still, faith words are somewhat different since they are minted in an experience of God and acquire the sense of eternity and the permanence of the divine. Like the Incarnate Word, faith words shine with both human and divine resonance. The experience of God is too precious to be forgotten or overly subject to human caprice.

This is why Jesus sent the Church the Holy Spirit to hover over religious language and help us treat it with care and reverence: "The Holy Spirit that the Father will send in my name—he will teach you everything and remind you of all that I told you" (Jn 14:26 NAB).

Of course we should distinguish the words of revelation in Scripture, which have a privileged place in religion, from other words that explain the insights into revelation acquired throughout the centuries. These explanatory words are servants of revelation and yet deserve inclusion in our faith tradition because of their fidelity to God's Word.

The editors urged me to think of this book as an inspirational dictionary so that an invitation to faith emerges from the context. I found this to be an appealing challenge and pondered numerous ways to lift the veil of the word so that God's voice could be heard. These hundreds of religious words, after all, are the outcome of centuries of prayerful use. Believers have taken them, sung them, spoken them, and polished them with the faith experience of generations.

Many of the words were fought over at Church councils, and echoes of those debates linger behind the precise shape they take on the page or in the ear. Other words recall momentous faith decisions that changed history, such as the Virgin Mary's "yes" to the angel Gabriel at the Annunciation. And then there are everyday words that tell the story of the unimpeded continuity of Catholic life through the centuries. Finally, the words of the Mass and the Liturgy of the Hours so strongly echo God's active presence that Catholics call them *lex credendi,* the very "law of believing."

Occasionally, when it seemed suitable I have offered a pointer for further study. I resisted the temptation to do this more often mainly because the nature of this work is more a record of Catholic word usage than a study guide that assumes the user has a more ambitious goal.

In conclusion I wish to thank Bert Ghezzi and Heidi Saxton of Servant Publications for their encouragement and the opportunity to produce this book. I also praise the Holy Spirit for his help, which I regularly sought and which was generously given.

A

Abba

We begin with God, from whom all blessings flow. While God is an infinite mystery, he has gradually revealed truths about himself. Jesus Christ, God's Son, is the greatest revelation of God's inner life. It is from Jesus we learn that God is our loving Father.

So caring and tender is the Father that we are invited to call him "Abba," which in English is close to speaking of him as "Daddy" (see Rom 8:15; Gal 4:6). Even when we are adults we may still address God with this childlike name to characterize our loving dependence upon him.

Abbey

An abbey is a monastery for monks, canons, or nuns, who belong to religious orders such as the Benedictines, Cistercians, Trappists, and Norbertines. Most of them follow the Rule of St. Benedict or the Rule of St. Augustine. Some abbeys are completely contemplative, while others combine contemplation with active ministry such as serving parishes or sponsoring schools and colleges.

All the members embrace a life consecrated to God and live by the evangelical counsels of poverty, chastity, and obedience. Their spirituality centers on the celebration of the Eucharist, the Liturgy of the Hours, and personal prayer. Each abbey is an independent institution, though it may form a network with other abbeys in a geographical region for the sake of advancing common interests.

Abbot

The major superior of an abbey of men is called the abbot. In the case of a nun's abbey, the major superior is an abbess. The term *abbot* means "father." Abbeys are meant to be monastic families that stress the primacy of community under the leadership of an abbot or abbess, who presents the members with Christ's call to holiness and helps them to achieve it.

Abortion

Any direct or intended choice to kill an unborn child, at any stage of the child's development in the womb, is an abortion. This is a gravely immoral act. Direct abortion is always wrong.

The Church has held this teaching with remarkable consistency in every age of its history. We should respect and protect unborn human life from the moment of conception. The unfolding of the child's life in the womb should always be linked to the loving concern of God, in whose image the child has been created.

Absolution

After the confession of sins in the sacrament of reconciliation, the penitent hears the priest recite the words of absolution from sins. Through the ministry of the priest, divine forgiveness enfolds the penitent, bringing freedom from sin and new graces to help the person continue the journey to salvation with renewed strength and enthusiasm.

Abstinence

On Ash Wednesday, the Fridays of Lent, and Good Friday, Catholics are expected to refrain or abstain from eating meat. This practice is meant to remind us of Christ's passion and death for our salvation. It is a simple form of self-discipline designed to motivate us toward a life of virtue.

Abstinence also refers to avoiding sexual activity until one enters marriage. Church-sponsored chastity programs for teens and young adults always include abstinence training as part of their process. Members of religious orders and congregations take the vow of chastity, in which they promise permanent abstinence from sexual activity.

Acts of the Apostles

Written by St. Luke, the Acts of the Apostles is a book of the Bible about the development of the early Church after the ascension of Christ. It is mainly about the acts (or actions) of St. Peter and St. Paul. The book contains historical scenes such as Pentecost, the first miracle of St. Peter and St. John, the conversion and journeys of St. Paul, the Council of Jerusalem, and other stories that illustrate the growing faith of the first Christians.

The description in Acts of the first Christian community—built around life in common, prayer, the sharing of goods, and the breaking of the Bread (the Eucharist)—has inspired the founding of numerous faith communities, both religious and lay, throughout history. Because the Holy Spirit figures so prominently in the book, some have called it "the Gospel of the Holy Spirit."

Adoration

Ever since human beings have been granted experiences of the beauty and majesty of God, their response has been loving and grateful adoration of the divine presence. We adore God alone. This act is the free and total submission of our whole being to God and his will.

Adoration is best acted out in our celebration of the Eucharist. In the Mass we adore the Father who calls us to worship, the Son who redeems us, and the Holy Spirit who sanctifies us. We extend this action when we spend time before the Blessed Sacrament in prayer and love. Our adoration assumes a practical outcome when we faithfully witness to Christ in love and service of others.

Adultery

When a married man or woman engages in sex with someone who is not his or her spouse, this sin is called adultery. It is expressly forbidden by the sixth commandment. God is the author of marriage and expects the husband and wife to enter into a lifelong, faithful relationship with each other. Adultery is an act of infidelity to a spouse. Its destructive consequences for a marriage are well known.

Spouses should thank God each day for the pledge of love they made to each other on their wedding day. The rings of fidelity they wear are symbolic reminders of the reality and promise of their love for each other.

Advent

Every year, in the four weeks before Christmas, the Church celebrates the season of Advent. These days mark the beginning of the Church's liturgical year. The word *advent* means "the coming." In Advent the Church calls us to meditate on the second coming of Christ at the end of time, his first coming at Bethlehem, and his present rebirth in our lives on the feast of Christmas.

The color purple is worn for liturgical celebrations to bring our attention to the penitential character of Advent. We are invited to reflect on our constant need for moral and spiritual conversion. In so doing, with God's help, we increase our capacity for receiving an increase of divine love, which we are then able to share with others.

Agnosticism

In one way or another, every human being is searching for God. The drive to find God is planted in the human heart. Many people have been blessed with the gift of faith and so have discovered God in his infinite riches. Others are on a longer journey and still searching. Among these are self-described agnostics.

The term means literally "not knowing." Agnostics say they do not know God, nor whether he exists. Generally, they are people sincerely looking for truth and meaning. Some do come to faith in God and some do not. We hope and trust that these men and women of goodwill may one day come to the precious gift of faith.

Alb

At liturgies the priest wears a long white robe called an alb. The word *alb* comes from the Latin for "white." Scripture has numerous descriptions of Old Testament temple priests that picture them wearing white linen robes.

All Saints' Day

On the first of November we celebrate the Feast of All Saints. We gather at the Eucharist to praise God for the victory of his grace in the lives of millions of people who remained faithful to him on earth. We recall how they loved God and people and served the needs of justice and peace.

The Church has canonized certain saints whose heroic virtue was a special grace in their time. On All Saints' Day we think of all those other good people who have also gone to heaven. They make us feel that we too can respond faithfully to the call to holiness.

All Souls' Day

On the second of November we have the Liturgy of All Souls. Some good people at the time of their death are not yet ready to enter heaven. They go to purgatory, where they receive the final graces of purification from the remains of their earthly sins. This prepares them to enjoy the beauty and glory of God with nothing standing in the way. By our Masses and prayers on earth we express solidarity with the souls in purgatory and beg God for the graces they yet need for their ultimate purification.

Almsgiving

The world is filled with the poor, the hungry, the naked, and those unjustly treated. This is true even in wealthy countries such as the United States. We are expected to help them in many ways, one of which is charitable giving—another name for almsgiving.

In his Last Judgment sermon, just before his death, Jesus taught that at the end of time we shall be judged on whether we have taken care of the poor and the needy (see Mt 25:31-46). Christ himself comes to us in these people. To serve them is to serve him, and so to be saved.

Altar

At the center of the sanctuary in every Catholic Church is the altar, a tablelike structure made of stone, marble, or wood. It is consecrated—that is, made holy—by a bishop. The altar is the most sacred part of a church because it is there that the sacramental celebration of the Eucharist takes place.

At the time of the altar's consecration, a relic of a saint is placed in its center. This connects the saint with the death and resurrection of Christ. The placement of the relic there illustrates the enduring power of the cross and of Easter as these are made present for us and our salvation in the Eucharistic celebration at the altar.

Angel

Sacred Scripture contains many stories about angels. The angel Raphael guided the young Tobit to a marriage with Sarah. The angel Gabriel told St. Zachary that his wife St. Elizabeth would bear a son. In the skies over Bethlehem, angels sang of God's glory the night Jesus was born. God created angels to bring divine messages to earth and to fill heaven with the music of the divine glory.

Angels are pure spirits with the capacity to think and love. While they have no bodies, they are sometimes given a human appearance when bringing a divine message to someone on earth. Each of us has a guardian angel to help us walk the path of salvation.

Angelus

The Angelus is a prayer meant to be said at noontime and at six in the evening. It is called Angelus because it recalls the role of the angel Gabriel appearing to Mary and inviting her to become the mother of the Son of God. In many places a church bell rings at noon and evening to call people to recite the Angelus prayers and renew their faith in the Incarnation of Jesus.

Annulments

Ordinarily, annulments pertain to the sacrament of marriage and state that no sacramental bond exists between two spouses in question. This declaration may be made for reasons such as lack of proper consent, the existence of an undisclosed obstacle, or psychological factors that prevent one or both parties from assuming the responsibilities of marriage. Annulments are received only after extensive investigation of the marriage by a Church tribunal.

Annunciation

St. Luke's Gospel contains the story of the coming of the angel Gabriel to ask the Virgin Mary to accept the call of God to be the mother of his Son (see Lk 1:26-38). The event is called the Annunciation because it was the announcing of this invitation to Mary. On March 25, the Church celebrates this Feast of the Annunciation of the Lord.

Mary asked the angel how this could happen since she had no sexual relations with a man. The angel told her that the Child would be conceived in her womb by the power of the Holy Spirit. Mary accepted this truth in faith.

The child was then conceived by the Spirit's power. Hence the incarnation of the Son of God began at this moment. Mary's faith-filled assent is a model for our own faith assent to God's will for us.

Anointing of the Sick

The sacrament of the anointing of the sick is meant for anyone who begins to be in danger of death due to sickness or old age. It may be repeated should the person recover and again become gravely ill. It may also be given before a serious operation.

The New Testament roots of the sacrament are found in Mark 6:13 and, more famously, in James 5:14-15. Bishops and priests are authorized to be ministers of this sacrament. Its benefits include graces of spiritual strength to trust in God, the healing of the soul in the forgiveness of sins, and sometimes the healing of the body—should that be God's will.

Antichrist

The term *antichrist* appears only in the first and second letters of St. John (see 1 Jn 2:18, 22; 4:3; 2 Jn 7). But the idea of the antichrist appears in other texts as well. St. Paul calls him the "lawless one" (see 2 Thes 2:3-12 NAB). The Apocalypse describes him as the "beast" (see Rv chapters 12–13). He will terrorize Christians prior to the second coming of Christ.

Apocalyptic passages in the Old Testament provide the origins for a belief in the antichrist. Prophets envisioned a final struggle between those faithful to God (Israel) and those hostile to him (pagan nations). This war will culminate in an epic struggle at the end of history. God will win the battle, which will be accompanied by cosmic signs and disturbances.

In eras of social instability and upheaval there is a tendency to believe the antichrist has appeared and history is about to end. Christ cautioned us, however, not to attempt to predict the date (see Mt 24:36).

Apocalypse

See **Revelation, Book of.**

Apocrypha

This word means "hidden" or "secret." It refers to books that were written in the style of texts in the Old and New Testaments and that claimed to be authentic Scripture, but in fact were not.

Apologetics

Ever since the emergence of heresies in the early Church there have arisen defenders of the faith. Apologetics is the name given to this defense of the faith. Contemporary apologetics deals with objections to the Catholic faith from groups such as fundamentalist Christians, Mormons, and Jehovah's Witnesses. There is also a Catholic apologetics aimed at cultural opposition to the faith.

The tools of apologetics include Scripture studies, Church history, authoritative Church teaching, and philosophy. In this last instance the relationship of faith and reason is paramount. Wherever possible, the principles of dialogue are invoked.

Apostate

An apostate is someone who has denied the major tenets of Catholic belief and is no longer in communion with the Church.

Apostles

Jesus called twelve special men to continue his mission of proclaiming the kingdom of God, salvation from sin, and the gift of divine life. They were Simon Peter, his brother Andrew, James the elder, his brother John, Phillip, Bartholomew, Matthew, Thomas, James the younger, Jude, Simon the zealot, and Judas Iscariot. Jesus appointed Peter their leader.

After the betrayal and death of Judas, the remaining apostles chose Matthias to take his place. Matthias had been with Jesus and the apostles all during Christ's ministry and was a witness to the resurrection. We say the Church is apostolic because she was built by Christ on the foundation of the apostles (see Eph 2:19-20).

Apostles' Creed

The Apostles' Creed is an authentic summary of the faith of the apostles. It was not written by them, but rather by someone in the Church of Rome at a very early period to serve as a creed to be recited by the newly baptized. Catholics, familiar with saying the Rosary, always begin it by praying the Apostles' Creed.

Apostolate

The whole Church is apostolic in the sense that all members of the Church are called to share their faith in Christ with others. Every baptized person is summoned to be an ambassador for Christ. This is the apostolate. The laity, according to their qualifications and circumstances, have a vocation to bring the gospel to the culture in which they find themselves. This is accomplished by witness, moral courage, and sharing faith whenever possible.

Apostolic Succession

The apostles wanted to make sure that the mission entrusted to them by Christ would continue after their deaths. So they ordained bishops from among their helpers to carry on and consolidate the work they had begun. The office that Christ confided to St. Peter alone was permanently passed on to his successors, the popes. The office that the apostles received for shepherding the Church endures, without interruption, in the sacred order of bishops.

Apparitions

Scripture records numerous visions or apparitions. Angels appeared to St. Zachary, Mary, and the shepherds. The book of Revelation records that St. John saw many visions of the heavenly liturgy and of angels.

In recent history apparitions of the Blessed Virgin have occurred at La Salette, Lourdes, and Fatima. When messages are given in the visions, they are called private revelations to subordinate them to Revelation, properly speaking, that is found in Apostolic Tradition and Scripture, and interpreted by the Magisterium. Approved private revelations are meant to support and strengthen our faith in God's public revelation given for our salvation and the gift of divine life.

Archangel

St. Paul writes that an archangel will sound a trumpet announcing the resurrection of the dead (see 1 Thes 4:16). An archangel is a member of the highest rank of angels, such as St. Michael the Archangel (see Jude 9).

Archbishop

Normally, this is the title of a bishop who administers an archdiocese, which is a local church that is generally large in size and historically significant. It is customary to cluster several dioceses into a province at whose center is an archdiocese. The archbishop, and the bishops of the associate dioceses in a province, work together collegially for the greater pastoral good of God's people.

Ascension of Christ

In the Acts of the Apostles, St. Luke describes the forty-day ministry of the risen Lord to his apostles and disciples. On the fortieth day, Jesus ascended into heaven. The account of the Ascension echoes the narrative of Christ's Resurrection.

While clouds of glory reflect the exaltation of Jesus, two angels appear, as had happened at the tomb. They advise the apostles to stop staring into the sky. Jesus has gone into glory, and they were to spend the next days in prayer for the coming of the Holy Spirit (see Acts 1:6-14).

Ash Wednesday

The forty days of Lent begin on Ash Wednesday. It is customary for a great many Catholics to go to church and have their foreheads marked with ashes. The ashes are made from the burning of palm branches from the previous year's Palm Sunday.

These ashes are blessed with words that ask God to help the people keep the Lenten season in preparation for the joy of Easter. The priest uses one of the following prayers when giving ashes: "Turn away from sin and be faithful to the gospel" or "Remember that you are dust and unto dust you will return."

Assumption of Mary

On August 15, the Church celebrates the Feast of the Assumption of Mary. The meaning of the teaching is well stated in the opening prayer: "All-powerful God, you raised the sinless Virgin Mary, the mother of your Son, body and soul, to the glory of heaven."

Faith in Mary's assumption dates to the earliest centuries of the Church and was confirmed in 1950 when Pope Pius XII declared the truth a dogma of faith.

Mary's unique gifts of being sinless, the mother of God, and ever a virgin account for the singular privilege of her assumption. Her participation in Christ's Resurrection confirms the promise of our own.

Atheism

People who deny God's existence are called atheists. Atheism may take many forms, such as a practical materialism that says this is all there is. Or it may say that humans alone run everything and are masters of their own destiny.

Atheism is an act against the first commandment and the virtue of religion. But the culpability of atheists can be diminished by their intentions and circumstances. Church members can occasion atheism by their careless practice of the faith and their religious and moral failures. On the other hand, an authentic gospel witness to love, justice, and compassion is an important antidote to atheism.

Avarice

The tenth commandment forbids the practice of avarice (or greed), which is a passion for money and the power it brings. St. Paul goes so far as to say that the love of money is the root of all evils (see 1 Tm 6:10). Selfless generosity cures avarice.

B

Baptism

Baptism is a sacrament that initiates a person into membership in the Church. Baptismal grace forgives original sin and all personal sins. It is the first sacrament that a Christian receives and it unites the candidate to Christ, who died for our sins and rose from the dead for our salvation. Baptism, confirmation, and the Eucharist make up what are called the sacraments of initiation.

The central ritual of baptism consists in either being immersed in water or having water poured on the head, while the celebrant says, "I baptize you in the name of the Father, and of the Son, and of the Holy Spirit." The ceremony takes place at the baptismal font or pool, which is situated in a prominent place in the parish church.

Basilica

In the days of the Roman Empire, a basilica was a large public building that housed courtrooms, stores, banks, and archives. Rectangular in shape, the basilica's central space was flanked by pillars separating it from side aisles. At the end of the building was an apse, or semicircular space.

During the years of persecution, when Christianity was forbidden a public presence, the Eucharist was celebrated in private homes. After Christianity became an approved religion, it was judged that the basilica style of building suited the needs of the Church's liturgy. A number of basilica churches were built throughout the Roman Empire. The best-known basilica is St. Peter's in Vatican City. Today the term basilica is a title of honor bestowed on certain churches because of their historical importance or as extraordinary centers of worship.

Beatific Vision

When people go to heaven they are granted the capacity to see God. This contemplation of God in his heavenly glory is called the beatific vision. Jesus promised this gift in one of the eight beatitudes, when he said that the pure in heart shall see God (see Mt 5:8). St. Augustine notes that we will be filled with perfect joy when we see God. The eternal happiness of heaven, flowing from the beatific vision, is called beatitude.

Beatification

In the Church's process of making a saint, beatification is the last step prior to canonization. Three steps are needed for beatification. The Office for the Cause of Saints must examine the candidate's life and judge it to be one of heroic virtue. The person's writings need to be reviewed and seen to be consistent with the Church's teachings. Finally, a miracle attributed to the intercession of the candidate must have occurred and been authenticated.

Beatitudes

At the beginning of his Sermon on the Mount, Jesus proclaims the eight Beatitudes (see Mt 5:1-12). These eight sayings constitute a charter for human happiness. They contain the Christian attitudes that should govern our moral and spiritual behavior.

The Beatitudes invite us to face experiences of mourning, injustice, poverty of spirit, persecution, purity, and peacemaking in a spirit of faith. When we unite these experiences to the love and passion of Christ, we are led to union with his resurrection. Properly lived, the Beatitudes open us to genuine happiness.

Benediction

This term applies to a popular Catholic devotion called Benediction of the Blessed Sacrament. In this ceremony the Eucharist is placed in a sacred vessel called a monstrance, where it can be seen and adored. Hymns are sung and prayers are said, and the Eucharist is reverenced with incense. Finally, the priest raises the monstrance and blesses the people. The ritual is meant to increase people's faith in the Eucharist and motivate them to appreciate the Mass more deeply.

Bible

Also called Sacred Scripture, the Bible contains the truths of God's revelation. The books of the Bible were composed by human authors under the inspiration of the Holy Spirit. In the Catholic Bible there are forty-six books of the Old Testament and twenty-seven books of the New Testament.

These books relate the history of salvation and teach us what we need to know and do in order to be saved from sin and receive the gift of divine life here and eternal life in heaven. Jesus Christ, the Son of God and son of Mary, is the heart of biblical revelation and the One who sheds light on its full meaning.

Birth Control

This is a popular name given to the practice of artificial contraception. The procedure involves the use of mechanical, medical, or chemical methods to stop conception from taking place as a result of sexual intercourse. The Church disapproves of this method because it interferes with the openness to procreation required by marriage and also with the goal of marital love. (The Church's position is explained more completely in the *Catechism of the Catholic Church*, par. 2366-72.)

Bishop

A bishop is one who has received the fullness of the sacrament of holy orders. Through his ordination he becomes a member of the college of bishops and a successor of the apostles. He is appointed the leader of a diocese and is called as a shepherd to teach, rule, and sanctify the people.

By his membership in the college of bishops he is expected, with them, to have solicitude for the worldwide apostolic mission of the Church. In many cases the diocesan bishop receives an assistant or auxiliary bishop to help him in his mission. He may also receive a coadjutor bishop who will succeed him when he leaves office.

Blasphemy

Language that abuses God and demonstrates contempt for him is called blasphemy. The second commandment forbids such defiant speech. It also prohibits the misuse of God's name to cover up or justify torture, murder, crimes, or injustices done to people. Blasphemy is contrary to the respect due to God.

Blessed Sacrament

The Holy Eucharist is often called the Blessed Sacrament. This title for the Eucharist is usually associated with the reserved Eucharist in the tabernacle and underlines our belief in the real presence of Christ.

Blessing

A blessing communicates God's help to individuals or an assembled community. Blessings are usually given by a priest. He makes the sign of the cross over us and asks the Father, Son, and Holy Spirit to bless us. One of the most beautiful blessing prayers in the Bible may be found in Numbers 6:24-27. A priest is sometimes asked to bless medals, statues, homes, boats, and other objects to impart to them a reminder of the divine protection and the help being sought.

Body of Christ

Scripture applies the expression "Body of Christ" to both the Eucharist and the Church. In the four accounts of the institution of the Eucharist (see Mt 26:17-29; Mk 14:12-25; Lk 22:7-20; 1 Cor 11:23-26), Jesus uses words over the bread that changes it into his Body. The sixth chapter of St. John's Gospel portrays Jesus conducting an extensive dialogue with the people about their need to partake of the bread of life that is his Body.

As for the use of this phrase to apply to the Church, we turn to St. Paul's first letter to the Corinthians (see 12:21-31). He uses the image of a head and members of a body to illustrate the intimacy of Christians with Christ. Jesus is head of the body of which Christians are the members (see also Col 1:18).

A number of other places in the New Testament support this imagery. It became one of the favorite images used by St. Augustine in his sermons and theological writing. The fathers of the Church loved to say that the Body of Christ as Eucharist builds up the body of Christ as Church.

Breaking of the Bread

The early Church described the Eucharistic celebration as "the breaking of the bread" (see Acts 2:42). At the Last Supper Jesus took bread, blessed it, *broke it,* and gave it to his disciples, saying, "This is my Body" (Mt 26:26).

On Easter night the risen Jesus walked with two disciples on the road to Emmaus, helping them to understand the crucifixion as the path to Christ's glory. When they arrived in Emmaus and sat down to eat with him, they recognized him in the breaking of the bread (see Lk 24:13-35). This is one of several titles given to the celebration of the Eucharist.

Breviary

This is an alternate name sometimes given to the four volumes of the Liturgy of the Hours, which is recited or sung daily by priests, monks, nuns, brothers, and a number of lay people.

Bride of Christ

This is an image of the Church found in several places in the New Testament (see 2 Cor 11:2; Rv 22:17). It is designed to help us realize the depth of the covenant Jesus has with the Church. This covenant comprises fidelity and love.

Jesus loves the Church absolutely and with unwavering fidelity. The Church in turn is called to return this love and fidelity with the joyful surrender of a bride. The letter to the Ephesians uses this imagery to inspire husbands and wives to love each other as Christ has loved his bride, the Church (see Eph 5:25-32).

Calling

God addresses a special calling to believers consistent with their gifts and the situation in which they find themselves. This is an expression of God's universal call to holiness. It includes the call to marriage, the single life, the priesthood, or the religious life, but it also refers to the invitation to be a teacher, a laborer, a businessperson, an artist, a farmer, a politician, a secretary, and so on.

The religious term for this calling is *vocation*. The believer's response is a faithful assent arrived at by God's grace, prayer, and discernment. See also **Vocation.**

Canon Law

The body of laws by which the Catholic Church is governed is called canon law. The term *canon* comes from the Greek word *kanon,* meaning a "measure" or "rule."

Canon of Scripture

The judgment rendered by the Church as to which books ought to be considered sacred Scripture resulted in what is known as the canon of Scripture. Historically, this complex process took many years. The Church sought to establish an authoritative list of biblical books.

Scholars in Old Testament times already had determined which books should be considered canonical. When faced with a number of writings from New Testament times, the Church needed to select those which also belonged in the Canon. Guided by the Holy Spirit and the wisdom that comes with the passage of time, the Church chose twenty-seven books for the New Testament and retained forty-six books for the Old Testament.

The Catholic canon differs slightly from the Orthodox, Protestant, and Jewish canons. (For further reading, see *The New Jerome Biblical Commentary,* 66:1-101.)

Canonization

The final step in the making of saints is called canonization. One miracle attributed to the intercession of the candidate after the time of beatification is necessary for sainthood. At a canonization the Church proclaims that the person is a saint, now in heaven and worthy of public honor and imitation. The faithful may seek the saint's intercession for their needs. They can name churches after the saint and celebrate liturgies that memorialize the saint.

Capital Sins

Often called the seven deadly sins, these evil acts give birth to other vices and sins. The capital sins are pride, greed, envy, anger, gluttony, lust, and sloth. Scripture says that greed, or the love of money, is the root of all other evils (see 1 Tm 6:10).

Cardinal

A cardinal is a major member of the Church's hierarchy and belongs to the College of Cardinals. Only cardinals who have not yet reached the age of eighty can elect a pope. Most cardinals are either archbishops of prominent archdioceses or heads of Vatican offices. Cardinals must be ordained priests at the time of their selection. Except in a few cases, cardinals are either already bishops or are consecrated bishop just prior to their elevation to the cardinalate.

Cassock

A cassock is a full-length black robe that may be worn by diocesan parish priests.

Catacombs

During the early centuries of Christianity in Italy, the faithful dug a maze of underground tunnels with niches in the walls—now known as the catacombs—where they buried their deceased relatives and friends. Some of these were martyrs whose graves were sites of veneration for these saints.

Catechesis

The explanation of the truths of the Catholic faith is called catechesis. It involves the building of a personal relationship with the Father, Son, and Holy Spirit, as well as learning the meaning of the teachings of Christ and the Church. Believers are expected to engage in a lifelong growth in union with Christ along with a persistent study of the truths of revelation so that they may come to full maturity in the faith.

Catechisms

The word catechism comes from a Greek term that means "to echo." Until the invention of the printing press, most cultures were oral societies. A religion teacher, called a catechist, would speak a teaching of the Church and instruct the listener to "echo" it— to repeat it until it was learned by heart. With the arrival of widespread literacy, printed catechisms with questions and answers for the users became the norm for learning religion.

Another kind of catechism was created in the year 1566 by the Council of Trent. It was called the *Roman Catechism*. Composed as a comprehensive, systematic presentation of the faith, it endured as source book for religion teachers until recent times. In 1992 the Church published the *Catechism of the Catholic Church* as a successor to the

Roman Catechism. Pope John Paul II has called this catechism a "sure norm of faith."

Catechumens

Converts seeking admission to the Catholic Church are called catechumens. The word comes from the Greek and means "instruction." Catechumens are enrolled in the Rite of Christian Initiation of Adults (RCIA), a process of teaching, rituals, and community building that prepares them for baptism, confirmation, and their first Communion at the Easter Vigil.

Cathedral

A cathedral is the central church of a diocese and is named after the chair (from the Latin *cathedra*) of the bishop, who is the chief presider at its liturgies. The cathedral is the place where the bishop ordains priests, blesses the holy oils, and celebrates other major liturgies. The pope, as Bishop of Rome, has his cathedral at St. John Lateran. Many cathedrals have become famous because of their history and architectural beauty, such as Notre Dame of Paris and the Duomo in Florence.

Catholic

The word *catholic* means "universal." As one of the four "marks" of the Catholic Church, it means that the Church is the sacrament of salvation for everyone. The Church has the fullness of the faith, all the sacraments, and apostolic succession. Sent by Jesus to all nations, commissioned to speak to the conscience of all peoples, the Church strives to relate to every nation and culture.

Celibacy

The vow to give up marriage and abstain from all sexual activity is called celibacy. Diocesan seminarians in the Latin Rite promise celibacy prior to being ordained to the diaconate. Members of male and female religious orders and congregations take the vow of chastity and so remain celibate and virginal. The purpose of celibacy is to give an undivided heart to the service of God and the Church and to witness to the kingdom of heaven in the midst of daily life.

Cenacle

The Upper Room where Jesus instituted the Eucharist at the Last Supper was called the cenacle. The word means "dining room." It was in that same cenacle that the descent of the Holy Spirit at Pentecost took place (see Acts 1:13). By extension, the term sometimes refers to rooms that are set aside for prayer.

Censer

The vessel used to contain heated charcoal and incense is called the censer. It is attached to chains that enable it to be carried and swung so it can emit the aromatic smoke from the burning incense in processions and at liturgies. The use of incense for worship is found in Jewish temple liturgy in biblical times and in Catholic worship throughout history. The rising of the incense smoke is a symbol of the worshipers' prayers going up to God.

Chalcedon, Council of

The fourth ecumenical council of the Church took place at Chalcedon in the year 451. The council fathers defined, as a matter of faith, that Jesus Christ is both fully God and fully man, being one divine Person in two natures. In his divine nature he is God. In his human nature he is a man. His one divine Person links the two natures together. A popular Catholic prayer at Benediction of the Blessed Sacrament recalls this teaching: "Blessed be Jesus Christ, true God and true man."

Chalice

The cup containing wine and used by the priest at Mass is a chalice. Usually made of some precious metal, the chalice holds the wine that is changed into the Blood of Christ at the Eucharist.

Chapel

The first chapel was a small building meant to house the cape of St. Martin of Tours (c. 316–97). St. Martin had vol-unteered to give his cloak to a freezing beggar, only to find out the beggar was Jesus in disguise. The enshrined cloak, or cape, gave its French name (*capelle*) to the building. Since then, small churches and private worship spaces have been customarily called chapels.

Chaplain

Originally, a chaplain was the priest assigned to a chapel. Gradually the term was applied to priests in special ministries outside a parish. Priests who serve in the military, or in hospitals, prisons, large convents, or for people with special needs are called chaplains. Certain other groups such as policemen and firemen often have part-time chaplains.

Charisms

The Holy Spirit imparts a wide variety of gifts, or charisms, to Christians for the sake of building up the Church. In his first letter to the Corinthinans (see chapters 12–14), St. Paul gives an excellent description of the charisms of the Spirit. He explains their purpose, meaning, and principle of interpretation. St. Paul emphasizes that the greatest gift—charism—is love and devotes all of chapter 13 to the beauty of this charism. Religious orders and congregations use the term charism to refer to the spirit and vision of their founder, which they explore when updating themselves for contemporary ministry.

Charity

The love of God and neighbor are the two greatest commandments given us by Christ. This love is also called charity. St. Paul has written Scripture's most eloquent praise and description of charity (see 1 Cor 13:1-13). People frequently speak of charity as acts that relieve the symptoms of poverty. See also **Love.**

Chastity

An act that enables one to refrain from any sinful use of sexuality is called the virtue of chastity. Everyone, whether married or single, is expected to be chaste, practicing the virtue that opposes the sins of lust and sexual misconduct. Members of religious orders and congregations take the vow of chastity, which means they promise to remain celibates. They are expected to remain chaste and avoid lust or any kind of sexual act.

Chasuble

The outer garment a priest wears at Mass is a chasuble. Its ancient antecedent was the *casula*, a full-bodied cloak that covered the body. As fashions changed and men came to wear smaller cloaks, the *casula* was retained by priests and worn as a liturgical vestment.

Cherubim

One of the nine choirs of angels, the cherubim are described in Ezekiel (see chapters 9–10) as attendants at God's throne. Their semihuman looks bear the faces of a man, a lion, an ox, and an eagle. God appointed them to exercise his power over the world. They also appear in the book of Revelation (see chapters 4–5).

Choir

Most parishes have a group of special singers who form their choir. The majority of such choirs are volunteers, but there may be hired professionals to conduct them or to supplement their talents. Some sing from choir lofts and others from spaces assigned to them near the altar. Generally, they help support congregational singing, enabling active participation in the liturgy by all present. Sometimes they sing sacred motets or other performance-type music.

Chrism

Every Holy Week the bishop consecrates holy oils to be used for baptisms, confirmations, ordinations, and the sacrament of anointing. The Church name for this oil is chrism. Normally olive oil is used, but vegetable or coconut oil can be substituted. Chrism symbolizes the Holy Spirit's action in the sacraments where it is used.

Christ

See **Jesus Christ.**

Christian

Followers of Jesus Christ are called Christians. The disciples of Christ were first called Christians in Antioch (see Acts 11:26). All Christians have received the Holy Spirit in baptism.

Christmas

The feast of the birthday of Jesus Christ in Bethlehem of Judea is called Christmas. The name comes from the medieval title "Christ's Mass" and is the most popular of all Church celebrations. On the other hand, the Sacred Triduum of Holy Thursday, Good Friday, and the Easter Vigil is considered to be the Church's most important feast.

Church

Derived from the Hebrew word *qahal,* meaning "a God-called community," the Church is the Christian community founded by Christ and manifested visibly at Pentecost by the Holy Spirit. Hence the Church does not come into existence by the consent of its members, but only by the intent and will of Christ. Vatican II's document on the Church says it is a mystery initiated and sustained by God, a gathering of God's people, a sacrament of salvation for the world, and a hierarchical organization that supports its teachings, stability, and continuity.

Ciborium

A number of Eucharistic hosts are always reserved in the tabernacle, both for Communion for the sick and to supplement what might be needed at the next Mass. These hosts are contained in a cuplike vessel called a ciborium. The word is based on a Latin term for food. The reserved Eucharist also serves as an opportunity for adoration and prayer by people after Mass.

Circumcision

The removal of the foreskin of the male sexual organ is circumcision. Among the Hebrew people of the Old Testament it was considered a sign of their covenant with God. Jesus himself was circumcised according to custom.

In New Testament times, as Gentiles were converted to the Church, an argument arose over whether they needed to be circumcised. A council met in Jerusalem to discuss the problem (see Acts 15). The participants concluded that because of Christ's new covenant, membership in God's people does not require circumcision. Baptism unites the convert to Christ's covenant and paschal mystery.

Clergy

The term *clergy* normally applies to priests, but it also refers to deacons and bishops.

Cloister

Contemplative religious orders such as the Carmelites and the Trappists live in a cloister, to which outsiders are rarely admitted. This private area extends to the dining room, sleeping quarters, library, workstations, and other rooms. The church or chapel is open to worshipers. Those who live in the cloister restrict themselves from leaving it or having any extensive contact with the outside world. See also **Contemplative Life**.

Coadjutor Bishop

When an assistant bishop is appointed to help the bishop of a diocese and is given the right of succession, he is called a coadjutor bishop.

Collections

The basket is passed at weekend Masses to have a collection for the needs and maintenance of the parish. Sometimes a second collection is taken up for special needs, such as the missions or alleviation of the victims of an earthquake or similar tragedy. The collection takes place at the Offertory, or offering time.

Collegiality

When Christ chose the twelve apostles, he formed them into a college or permanent institution with St. Peter at the head. The bishops, together with the pope at their head, are the successors of St. Peter and the apostles and form a college like theirs. They work together to promote the mission of the Church. Strictly speaking, collegiality describes the manner in which the bishops exercise authority in communion with the Church and with the pope at their head.

Colors, Liturgical

The color of the vestments used by the priest at Mass is governed by the requirements of the liturgical seasons and feasts. Purple is used in Advent and Lent, except for the third Sunday of Advent and the fourth Sunday of Lent, when rose is used. White is used for feasts of Christ and Mary, the seasons of Christmas and Easter, and the feasts of angels and saints who were not martyrs.

Red is selected for Palm Sunday, Good Friday, and feasts of the apostles (except John), evangelists, and martyrs. Green is chosen for Ordinary Time. For funerals and Masses for the dead, white, purple, or black may be used.

Commandments

When asked which commandment was the greatest, Jesus replied that love of God and love of neighbor constitute the greatest commandments (see Mt 22:36-40). In another case, a rich young man came to Jesus and asked him what he needed to do to gain eternal life. Jesus told him to keep the commandments (see Mt 19:16-19). Jesus was referring to the Ten Commandments (or Decalogue) given by God to Moses at Mount Sinai (see Ex 20:2-17; Dt 5:6-21).

The first three of these Ten Commandments speak of how to love God. The last seven tell how to love our neighbor. Each commandment speaks against an evil and for a virtue.

God's commandments are designed to help people attain human fulfillment as well as union with God. There are also six precepts of the Church that give pastoral applications of the commandments (see the *Catechism,* par. 2041-43).

Communion, Holy

Receiving the Body and Blood of Christ in the Eucharist is the meaning of Holy Communion. In a broader sense it points to our union with other baptized Christians in the Church through the grace of Jesus. The Body of Christ in the Eucharist promotes communion with all members of the Church.

Communion of Saints

The spiritual union of all the redeemed in heaven, purgatory, and on earth form the communion of saints, a truth affirmed in the Apostles' Creed. Pastorally, this means that a vast outreach of love and concern flows among the entire community of the saved, not just for each other but for the salvation of all people as well. The teaching forms the basis of prayer to the saints for their intercession, of prayer for the liberation of the souls in purgatory, and of prayer for the needs of each other here on earth.

Community

The life of the Holy Trinity is marked by a community of love. Through the works of creation and redemption, the Holy Trinity calls the members of the Church to reflect divine community in their human community. The very first description of the Church after its manifestation at Pentecost was in terms of an ideal community (see Acts 2:42-47).

Because of sin, which divides people, the struggle to make community happen will always be a challenge. But the Holy Spirit, Source of love and community, constantly helps us with graces to accomplish this ideal. The Eucharist, the sacrament of unity, gives us incomparable food for this journey.

Concelebration

When other priests besides the main celebrant join in celebrating the Eucharist, we have concelebration.

Conclave

The assembly of cardinals, gathered for the election of a pope, is a conclave, from the Latin word for "with a key," meaning the electors work behind locked doors in strict secrecy. This takes place in the Sistine Chapel at the Vatican. A series of votes takes place until an election occurs. When the burned ballots reveal white smoke, people waiting for the news know that a new pope has been elected.

Concupiscence

Baptism takes away original sin but not all the damage done to the soul. An inclination to sin remains, and this is concupiscence. Nevertheless, the baptized person is also a redeemed image of God and has numerous sources of spiritual strength available through the sacraments, the presence of the Holy Spirit, prayer, the example and support of the community, and the life of the virtues.

Conference of Bishops

The bishops of a given country form a national organization of their members into a Conference of Bishops. They do this to find more effective ways to deepen the faith of the people, provide mutual support for themselves, strengthen unity with the universal Church, and deal with issues of Church and state.

Confession

Also called the sacrament of reconciliation, confession is a sacrament instituted by Christ for the forgiveness of sins and meant to reconcile the penitent with Christ and the Church. This sacrament has three parts: the confession of sins; the absolution by the priest in the name of Christ and the Church; and the satisfaction (or penance) given for the sake of helping the penitent in the process of moral and spiritual conversion.

Confession may be made in a reconciliation room or in a more private setting known as a confessional. It can also occur in a sick room or some emergency setting. The penitent is encouraged to return with peace and joy to the faith journey toward heaven.

Confirmation

The second of the three sacraments of initiation, confirmation seals a believer with the Holy Spirit (by means of holy oil, or chrism) and is usually performed by a bishop. At the Easter Vigil, the local priest administers confirmation to those coming into full communion with the Church. It is a sacrament of spiritual maturity that enriches the soul of the recipient with the deep graces of the Spirit.

Confirmation is administered for different age groups depending on local traditions. In the Eastern Rite, the sacrament is given to infants along with baptism. Elsewhere, it may be given to young children, teens, or adults according to custom. Confirmation calls the recipients to witness courageously to the faith.

Confiteor

At the beginning of Mass, the people are summoned to reflect on sins and faults that need forgiveness. This reflection is followed by various penance prayers, one of which is the confiteor, which means "I confess." This rite of penance is concluded by a prayer for forgiveness. While the confiteor is not the sacrament of confession, it is a suitable way to prepare for participation in the Eucharist.

Confraternity of Christian Doctrine (CCD)

The Church has always sought ways to train young people in the message and mission of Christ and the Church. The CCD has been one of the principal ways created to make this happen. In recent times diocesan and parish leaders prefer to speak of this ministry as religious education.

The primary audience for religion training is parish students from public elementary and secondary schools. They are prepared for first confession, first Communion, and confirmation, as well as for an understanding of the teachings of the faith. They are helped to have beliefs, attitudes, and practices that will make them active Catholics in their parishes and at liturgy, as well as moral and spiritual witnesses to faith in society. Religious education (CCD) also emphasizes adult education so that faith growth will develop throughout a person's life.

Conscience

The moral judgments we make about right and wrong behavior come from our conscience. "Let your conscience be your guide" is sound Catholic teaching. Conscience should be informed by the teachings of the Church, supported by communion with divine and human truth, and fed by a spirituality that flows from the Eucharist and the maternal mediation of our Blessed Mother.

Consecration

The vast influence of a secular culture tends to hide the reality of the sacred. The act of consecration makes sacred certain persons, places, and things. It awakens the sense of the sacred in an otherwise secular milieu.

Religious men and women who take vows enter consecrated life. Their witness in a community of love, obedience, chastity, and poverty is a powerful illustration of the sacred.

In a broad sense all the sacraments confer on the recipients a consecration, a making holy of persons by bringing them closer to God. It is also customary to consecrate churches and shrines, which then become holy ground, communicating the awe of God and inclining people to move toward the holy.

Consistent Life Ethic

The Church defends life from conception until death. Her position is consistent about the defense of human life in a number of critical situations. Hence the Church wants to protect the life of the unborn, seek peace in the world, defend the prisoner from capital punishment, stand up for the rights of workers, and walk with those near death lest someone wish to inflict on them a physician-assisted suicide or some other form of euthanasia.

Consistory

When the pope gathers the college of cardinals together to determine who should become new cardinals, the assembly is called a consistory. The term also applies to the ceremony in which the pope raises new men to the office of cardinal.

Contemplative Life

A life in which the primary goal is the contemplation of God by means of prayer, meditation, silent reflection, asceticism, and voluntary withdrawal from everyday life in the world is called the contemplative life. A number of orders of men and women such as the Carmelites and Trappists are committed to the contemplative life. But all religious orders and congregations practice some form of contemplative prayer even as they engage in active Church ministry.

Bishops, parish priests, and laity are invited to practice contemplative prayer as well and to be open to the gifts of deeper spirituality. All pastoral activity in the Church needs the support of contemplative prayer.

Contrition

Sorrow for sins, or contrition, is one of the necessary attitudes for a good confession. Implicit in contrition is the purpose of amendment—a resolve, with God's help, not to commit the same sin again.

Convent

The building where nuns or religious sisters live is called a convent.

Conversion

Profound changes in one's personal life, such as becoming a Christian and leaving behind a life of unbelief in Christ or his teachings, is an example of conversion. There are also conversions among Christians from a life of sin to a life of grace and virtue. Famous stories of conversions such as those of St. Paul, St. Augustine, Thomas Merton, and Dorothy Day dramatically describe the conversion process and serve as inspiration for other potential converts.

Cope

At Benediction of the Blessed Sacrament or in Corpus Christi processions, the priest wears an ankle-length cloak called a cope.

Corporal

From the Latin word for "body," the corporal is a square piece of linen placed on the center of the altar. Upon it rest the chalice of wine changed into Christ's Blood and the paten bearing the bread changed into Christ's Body.

Corporal Works of Mercy

In his sermon on the Last Judgment, Jesus describes the kinds of deeds that will bring eternal reward to those who practice them (see Mt 25:31-46). When we serve the needy we serve Christ. For teaching and practical purposes these desirable acts have been put in a list as follows: feed the hungry, shelter the homeless, clothe the naked, visit the sick and imprisoned, give water to the thirsty, struggle for human rights and freedom for hostages, and bury the dead. These are called corporal works of mercy because they deal with people's physical needs.

Corpus Christi

The feast of Corpus Christi occurs on the Sunday after Trinity Sunday. It originated in the Middle Ages as one of the pastoral responses to a decline in belief in the real presence of Jesus in the Eucharist. In addition to the Mass, the feast is often celebrated by a public procession through the streets near the church. The Blessed Sacrament is carried in a monstrance to the accompaniment of hymns and prayers. Sometimes there are stations where the procession stops and Benediction of the Blessed Sacrament is held.

Council

See **Ecumenical Councils.**

Counter-Reformation

The Church responded to the Reformation in the Counter-Reformation. The instrument for this inner reform as well as the theological replies to the objections of the Protestants was the Council of Trent (1545–63). The newly founded Society of Jesus (the Jesuits) and the Oratorians of St. Phillip Neri were among the outstanding groups leading the Counter-Reformation.

Today's ecumenical movement has initiated dialogues with the major Reformation churches, such as the Lutherans, Anglicans, and Presbyterians. Rather than continue the disputes of the past, the desire now is to seek Christian unity.

Covenant

Throughout the Old Testament there are covenant scenes between God and Israel, the most prominent being the one that took place at Mount Sinai (see Ex 19:3-6). In all covenant events, God takes the initiative, performing acts of liberation and love for his people, as when he freed Israel from Egyptian slavery. God then asks the people to enter into a lasting relationship with him, one based on faith, trust, and love.

After establishing the Sinai covenant, God gave the people the Ten Commandments so they would know how to live the consequences of the covenant. The final covenant was created by Jesus Christ at the cross and in the Resurrection, giving us the greatest imaginable gift of divine love: salvation from sins and the gift of divine life here and eternal life hereafter. The Holy Eucharist is a daily celebration of this covenant.

Creation

The creation accounts are found in the book of Genesis (see chapters 1 and 2). God created the world and all it contains out of nothing. The principal motive for creation was divine love, for God wanted to share his love with us.

The Church's teaching about creation is not the same as creationism, which discounts various scientific and evolutionary explanations of how the world came into being. We can agree with the creationists that God created the world. We can also find merit in the scientific efforts to explain the world's origin and development so long as we posit that God is the Author of creation and the continuing Presider over its development through divine provi-

dence. Finally, we hold that God is the creator of each human soul when a person is conceived. The Bible teaches us how to go to heaven, not necessarily how the heavens go.

Creeds

Summaries of Catholic belief were developed in the early centuries of the Church to clarify what should be believed. The Apostles' Creed was created at Rome, probably in the third century, as a statement of belief to be used in the rites of preparation for baptism. The Nicene Creed was produced after the Councils of Nicaea (325) and First Constantinople (381).

People begin the Rosary with the Apostles' Creed. All worshipers pray the Nicene Creed at Sunday liturgies. These doctrinal summaries provide the foundations of Catholic belief and practice.

Cremation

The burning to ashes of the bodies of the deceased is called cremation. The Church permits cremation, but asks that the body be brought to the Church in a coffin for the funeral, after which the cremation may take place. The cremains (ashes) should be put in a suitable urn and buried or stored in a place where the departed person's remains can be reverenced in anticipation of the resurrection of the dead at Christ's second coming.

Cross

The central symbol of Christianity is the cross upon which Jesus was crucified for our salvation. Most Catholics portray the crucified Christ on the cross so that his sacrificial love may always be seen. This cross is known as a crucifix. Protestants emphasize the cross without the figure of the crucified, pointing to the truth that Jesus is no longer on the cross, but risen from the dead. In any case, the cross and Easter form one paschal mystery.

Crozier

The vertical staff, curved at the top, is one of the symbols of office used by a bishop. The crozier stems from the staff of a shepherd and is meant to symbolize the pastoral care that a bishop is expected to exercise toward the people of his diocese. Croziers range in style from gold staffs decorated with jewels and some sculptures to simple wooden staffs.

Crucifix

See Cross.

Cruets

The small pitchers used to hold water and wine at Mass, cruets provide the elements needed for the chalice as well as water for washing the priest's hands.

Crypt

Sometimes large churches have an upper church and a lower one, which may be called the crypt, a Latin word for "cave." The term is also used for burial vaults.

Cult

The term *cult* has several meanings. It may be used as a name for worship, though this is rare. It can be employed to describe the devotions that develop to honor a saint. It may also refer to sects and organizations that impose enormous demands on their members, threatening them with punishments and psychological pain—and sometimes leading to mass suicides. The fatal flaw of this kind of cult is the total loss of respect for the person and freedom.

Curate

The assistant priest in the parish used to be called the curate. Today he is more likely to be named the parochial vicar or associate pastor.

Curia

The various agencies and their members who assist the pope in the governing of the Church comprise what is called the Curia. At the heart of the Curia are the ten Congregations, each presided over by a cardinal. There are also pontifical councils and commissions that deal with special developments and needs in the

Church. Dioceses have similar structures to address the needs of the local
church.

Cursillo

Literally meaning a "little course," the
Cursillo is a powerful tool for developing lay spirituality. The goal is to restore
the world to Christ. Participants in this
"short course in Christianity" strive to
acquire the mind of Christ and to live
in and by his presence.

Cursing

Some think of cursing mainly as the
thoughtless use of vulgar language, but
most see it as the unjustified and irrev-
erent use of the name of God and Jesus
Christ. Properly speaking, cursing is the
invocation of God's damnation and
destruction on people and places, and it
should be avoided.

Day of the Lord

In the Old Testament the teaching about "the day of the Lord" started with Israel's hope that God would take vengeance on the nation's enemies at the judgment (see, for example, Zep 1:2-18). Then the prophets taught that Israel too would be subject to God's judgment. With the arrival of Jesus Christ it became clearer that the kingdom of God, and the salvation he brought, was the real "day of the Lord" (see Acts 2:14-21). The final manifestation of the day of the Lord will happen at the second coming of Christ, which will include the judgment and the transformation of the world into a new heaven and a new earth (see Rv 21–22).

Deacon

As the New Testament Church grew, the apostles needed help in caring for the widows and other needy people (see Acts 6:1-7). The apostles chose seven suitable men, prayed over them, and laid hands on them. These were the first ordained deacons.

The order of diaconate continues to this day. Men on their way to priesthood are first ordained *transitional* deacons. We also have *permanent* deacons, who usually do not go on to priesthood. Most are married and serve local parishes as deacons for liturgies and other needs. They preach homilies, baptize, witness marriages, and conduct Christian burial services, but do not celebrate Mass.

Deaconess

Women have always been helpers in the work of the Church. In the early Church, some of them were called deaconesses. They were selected from among widows and had to be forty years or older. One of their major tasks was to help with the baptism of women converts when immersion in water was the custom. When questioned about the sacramental role of deaconesses, the Council of Nicaea (325) judged that they did not receive ordination.

Dead Sea Scrolls

In 1947, ancient scrolls were discovered in the caves of Qumran near the Dead Sea. These Dead Sea scrolls are remains from a library belonging to a community of Essenes that was founded about a century before Christ. The scrolls were stored in jars and hidden in these caves. They contain sections of most Old Testament books, some biblical commentaries, and copies of rules and customs practiced by the Essenes.

Until this discovery, the oldest copies

of Old Testament manuscripts dated to the tenth century. Finding texts that are a thousand years older has provided scholars with better tools for establishing more accurate renditions of the Old Testament. See also **Essenes**.

Death

The end of individual life on earth is death. Death causes anxiety, not only because of the pain and the gradual breakdown of the body, but also because of the dread of ceasing to exist. A deep intuition moves people to reject the thought of the total loss of self and personhood. All people bear within themselves the seed of eternity. Modern medicine has prolonged the life span but does not subdue the fears that accompany inevitable death.

Divine revelation teaches there is life beyond the grave. Scripture points out that death resulted from sin (see Rom 5:21; 6:23; Jas 1:15). On the other hand, Christ has freed man from death by his death and resurrection (see 1 Cor 15:56-57). This means that death is not the end of our life. The liturgy proclaims that at death, life is *changed*, not taken away.

Decalogue

See **Commandments**.

Dedication of a Church

A church building is consecrated in a ritual known as the Dedication of a Church. The rites picture the structure as an image of the universal Church built of the living stones of God's baptized people. The ritual includes the Litany of the Saints, the prayer of dedication, anointing of the altar and the walls, incensing the altar and people, placing a cloth on the altar, lighting of the candles on the altar and walls, celebration of Mass, and enshrining the Eucharist in the tabernacle.

Defender of the Faith

St. Peter teaches that we should have an explanation for the faith that is in us (see 1 Pt 3:15). Defending the faith has been going on ever since objections to the faith have arisen.

England's King Henry VIII (1509-47) wrote a response to Lutheran challenges in his book *An Assertion of the Seven Sacraments*. For the king's efforts, Pope Leo X awarded Henry the title "Defender of the Faith." Sadly, Henry later broke with the pope and the Catholic Church, starting his own Church of England. Pius XI named Gilbert K. Chesterton "Defender of the Catholic Faith" in 1936 for his outstanding writings on behalf of Catholicism. See also **Apologetics**.

Deification

In the Eastern Churches the process of salvation is called deification—being transformed more and more into the likeness of God. Christ's redemption takes away our sins and imparts divine life to us. St. Peter calls this a participation in the divine nature (see 2 Pt 1:4). This spiritual transformation is a lifelong process.

Deism

In the eighteenth-century cultural movement known as the Enlightenment, many of the intellectual leaders of this "Age of Reason" embraced a religion called Deism. They believed in God and agreed that he created the universe and the laws by which it was run. But they concluded that he left it alone and turned the running of the world over to people.

One of them compared God to a clockmaker who wound up the clock and set it free to run on its own. Hence there was no need for revelation, faith, miracles, grace, or any other means by which God would be involved in the world and human life. In fact, Thomas Jefferson, a prominent Deist, actually composed a copy of the Gospels in which Christ's miracles, baptism, transfiguration, and resurrection were removed. The Jesus that remained was simply a wisdom teacher, not a savior.

Deism survives today in new forms, such as some versions of secular humanism.

Demon

See **Devil**.

Deposit of Faith

St. Paul's second letter to St. Timothy refers to the truths of faith he has handed on. He expects St. Timothy to guard this rich trust with the Spirit's help (see 2 Tm 1:13-14). This is a reference to the deposit of faith, a body of saving truths of faith, which Jesus entrusted to the apostles, who handed them on to the Church. It is contained in Apostolic Tradition and Scripture. The Magisterium proposes this deposit of divinely revealed truths as the content of faith.

Descent into Hell

The Apostles' Creed says that Christ descended into hell after his death. This is not the hell of the damned, but rather the realm of the just who died before Christ's redeeming act. Jesus went there as a Savior, proclaiming the good news of salvation to them (see 1 Pt 3:18-19). In the Liturgy of the Hours, the Office of Readings for Holy Saturday contains a vivid homily by an unknown author from the early Church describing this joyful mission of Christ to the souls of the just.

Desecration of a Church

Acts that show grave disrespect for a church building, offending the faith of the Catholic community, desecrate the building. The response to this act is the Rite of Penitential Reparation, conducted by the bishop.

Desire, Baptism of

The Holy Spirit offers everyone the possibility of salvation. People who do not know the gospel of Christ and his Church, but seek the truth and do God's will within their understanding of it, can be saved. The assumption is that they would have *desired baptism* had they known of its need.

Despair

People who cease to hope that God can save them, help them toward redemption, or forgive their sins are in the state of despair. This loss of hope is contrary to God's love and mercy, for he is faithful to his promises to save us. Despair should not be confused with emotional traumas and psychological anxieties that reduce and even remove a person's responsibility or capacity to make a proper judgment.

Detraction

Unfair assaults on another's reputation and character by word or deed is known as detraction.

Development of Doctrine

The meaning of God's revelation in Tradition and Scripture has unfolded throughout the history of the Church. Guided by the Holy Spirit, the contemplative faith of the people, the reflection of theologians, and the Church's liturgy, the Magisterium teaches the deeper

meaning of the doctrines. Sometimes this is stimulated by forceful objections to truths of faith, such as the fourth-century Arian contention that Christ was not divine. Several councils of the Church convened to respond to this challenge and expressed in greater depth the ancient ecclesial faith in Christ's divinity (see *Catechism*, par. 94).

Devil

Scripture and Tradition teach that the devil or Satan is a fallen angel (see Jn 8:44; Rv 12:7-9). God created all the angels good. But the devil and other demons sinned and became fallen angels (see 2 Pt 2:4).

Scripture testifies that Satan tempts people to defy God and even tried to dissuade Jesus from his mission (see Mt 4:1-11). Jesus came, however, to destroy the works of the devil (see 1 Jn 3:8). Satan is powerful, but not infinitely so. God permits him to tempt us, but we are always free, with the help of grace, to reject him. See also **Lucifer.**

Devil's Advocate

In a canonization process, the person appointed to pose objections to making a candidate a saint is called the Devil's Advocate.

Devotion

Today, devotion is more likely to be spoken of as *commitment* to the call of

Christ and the Church to live out the consequences of our faith and worship. But devotion may also be understood as a special attraction to Our Lady, another saint, or an aspect of Christ's teaching, such as his divine mercy. This devotion normally involves some pious practice such as a litany, set prayers, a pilgrimage, or some other way of expressing affection and faith.

Diabolical Possession

When a demon or devil takes control of a person or his body, this is a case of diabolical possession. The Gospels report such instances (see Mk 5:1-20; Mt 8:28-34; Lk 8:26-39). Christ's exorcisms freed people from the domination of demons. Jesus taught that he drove out demons by the Spirit of God, and this meant that the kingdom of God would defeat that of Satan (see Mt 12:24-29).

While there are examples of possession today, they need to be distinguished from psychological illnesses. In the matter of a genuine possession, it should be noted that God never allows the devil to destroy a person's freedom. A person is always free to reject the demon's advance. See also **Exorcism**.

Diaspora

Throughout Jewish history, many families were driven into exile because of military conquests. The Jewish communities in foreign lands were called the Diaspora, a word that means "exile."

Didache

Written around A.D. 60, the *Didache* ("the teaching") is a book that contains Christian moral teachings, a description of baptismal and Eucharistic celebrations, instructions on the role of bishops and deacons, norms for discipline, and a prophecy about the end of the world. It presents a valuable picture of a developing Christian Church. The book was well known in the early Church and influenced the Fathers. The version of the full text now in use, dating from 1056, was discovered in 1873 at a monastery in Constantinople.

Dies Irae

The Black Plague ravaged Europe in the last half of the fourteenth century, killing a third of the population. People wondered whether the end of the world was coming and treated the plague as a sign of God's wrath. An unknown poet wrote the poem *"Dies Irae"* ("Day of Wrath") to reflect the apocalyptic anxieties of that age. It was set to music in Gregorian chant and sung at funerals until recent times. Perhaps its most famous musical settings are those composed by Mozart and Verdi.

Diocese

The universal Church is organized into geographical territories known as dioceses. Since Vatican II they are also called local churches to emphasize the communal nature of the Catholic identity. A diocese is led by a bishop and served mainly by diocesan priests as well as some priests from religious orders or congregations.

Exceptions to the territorial diocese are military dioceses, which minister to Catholics doing temporary duty in various places around the world. Another exception has to do with Catholics who belong to various Eastern Rites. They also have geographical lines, but these are usually broader than a given Latin Rite diocese.

Discalced

St. Francis and St. Clare introduced for their religious communities the ascetic practice of not wearing shoes, making them discalced or "unshod." Today this is a practice of religious orders and congregations who require sandals rather than shoes. The Discalced Carmelites are among those who follow this penitential custom.

Disciple

Students learn lessons from their teachers. Disciples follow their masters, committed to the person as well as the message. Jesus chose twelve apostles and seventy-two disciples. He expected them to hear the Word of God and keep it.

When told that his mother wanted to see him, Jesus said that his mother is someone who hears God's Word and practices it (see Mt 12:46-50). Mary did this more than anyone. At the foot of the cross stood Mary, the greatest disciple, and St. John, the "beloved disciple" (see Jn 19:26).

Dispensation

Exceptions to the laws of the Church are dispensations from the norm. Dispensations do not deal with God's laws, only with ecclesiastical ones.

Divine Office

See **Liturgy of the Hours.**

Divine Praises

After the blessing with the Eucharist at Benediction, a series of praise prayers called the Divine Praises are said. These have been in use since the eighteenth century and have been modified and added to over the years.

Divinity of Christ

The Son of God became the man Jesus Christ, conceived by the Holy Spirit in the womb of the Virgin Mary. In a variety of ways the New Testament affirms the divinity of Christ. At the baptism and transfiguration of Christ, the Father says that Jesus is his beloved Son (see

Mk 9:2-8). St. John's Gospel begins with a description of the Word of God becoming flesh in Christ (see Jn 1:1-18). St. Paul sings a hymn about how Christ, in the form of God, emptied himself of the status of glory and became a man and died for our salvation. Therefore, he insists, everyone should confess that Jesus is Lord—that is, God (see Phil 2:5-11).

The first four ecumenical councils of the Church defended the divinity of Christ against the Arian denial of this truth. Because he was divine, Christ's human acts acquired the power to save us from sin and give us divine life.

Divorce

Jesus spoke against divorce, arguing that God is the Author of marriage and did not want the bond to be broken (see Mt 19:3-9). The indissoluble bond of marriage entered into validly by a man and woman cannot be broken. A civil divorce does not break a valid marriage before God, hence remarriage is not permitted.

A divorced couple, not remarried, can still be in communion with the Church and welcome to the sacraments under the usual conditions. Many parishes reach out in compassion to the divorced to help them through the trauma that accompanies the breakdown of a marriage and family. See also **Annulments**.

Doctor of the Church

Certain outstanding teachers of the faith have been honored with the title Doctor of the Church. In a special way Saints Ambrose, Augustine, Jerome, Chrysostom, Athanasius, and Basil are known by this title. A number of other teachers from later centuries also have this title, including three women: Saints Catherine of Siena, Teresa of Avila, and Thérèse of Lisieux.

Dogma

Truths revealed by Christ and held by the Church's Magisterium are called dogmas. Members of the Church are expected to accept these truths of divine revelation as a matter of faith.

Dominicans

St. Dominic founded the Dominican Order of men in 1215. The order also has contemplative nuns and numerous congregations of religious sisters.

Dormition of the Blessed Virgin Mary

The death of Mary is often called her "going to sleep" or dormition, implying she would very soon awake and be assumed into heaven. The Church of the Dormition in Jerusalem commemorates her Assumption, as do the feasts of the Dormition in the Eastern Church. See also **Assumption of Mary**.

Doxology

The Greek word *doxa* means "glory,"
hence a doxology is a hymn or prayer
giving glory to the Father, Son, and
Holy Spirit. Traditionally, a doxology of
praise and adoration concludes the
praying of each psalm in the Liturgy of
the Hours, as well as in most of the
Church's hymns.

Dulia

From a Greek word for "reverence,"
dulia describes the respect Catholics
give to Mary, the other saints, and the
angels. It is not the same as the adoration given to God alone. *Dulia* is similar to the honor we give to national
heroes and heroines. The difference is
that we believe we can pray to Our
Lady, the other saints, and the angels to
intercede on our behalf with God. See
also **Hyperdulia**.

Dying, Prayers for the

The Catholic Church is a community, a
family called into being by the will of
the Father, the work of the Son, and
the abiding presence of the Spirit. As
with any family, God's people want to
accompany in love and prayer those
who are dying and preparing themselves
for the passage into eternal life. See also
Anointing of the Sick.

E

Easter

The greatest of all the Christian feasts, Easter celebrates the resurrection of Jesus Christ from the dead on the third day after his crucifixion. St. Bede the Venerable claims the name came from the word *Eastre*, a pagan Germanic goddess of spring. St. Paul teaches that Christ's resurrection is so essential that without it our faith would be useless (see 1 Cor 15:13-14).

Christ's death and resurrection form one saving event known as the *paschal mystery*. His death rescues us from our sins and his rising brings us divine life. The event is called *paschal* because it is Christ's ultimate fulfilling of the *Passover* experience of Israel, in which the angel of death spared the firstborn children during the tenth plague, and the people crossed the Red Sea away from slavery and toward freedom. Calvary and Easter form the new Passover by which we are saved from the slavery of sin and cross through the "sea" of baptism into the freedom of grace in Christ's kingdom.

At the Easter Vigil it is customary for candidates coming into full communion with the Church to have the sacraments of initiation (baptism, confirmation, the Eucharist).

Eastern Churches

There are five patriarchal sees designated by the ancient cities from which they originated: Jerusalem, Antioch, Alexandria, Constantinople, and Rome. Historically, the first four were called the Eastern Churches, and Rome headed the Western Church. Among the Eastern Churches developed from the four patriarchal sees are the Maronites, Chaldeans, Coptics, Armenians, and Byzantines, the last of which embrace the Greek, Russian, Melkite, Georgian, Ruthenian, and Ukrainian Churches and a number of others. Numerically, the Western Church is the largest.

During the theological controversies over the nature of Christ that took place in the Church's early centuries, the Maronite, Chaldean, Coptic, and Armenian communions adopted doctrinal positions contrary to those of various ecumenical councils, leading to their separation from the Catholic Church. In 1054, the Byzantine Church broke from Rome and is now known as the Orthodox Church.

Since 1596, a number of members of Eastern Orthodox Churches have sought and achieved reunion with Rome. Though once again fully a part of the Catholic Church, they have retained their unique liturgical rites and ecclesial traditions. Meanwhile, Rome and the still-separated Eastern Churches maintain an active dialog for the purpose of reaching ecclesial unity. See also **Orthodox Church.**

Eastern Monasticism

In the middle of the fourth century, St. Anthony of Egypt created the beginnings of eastern monasticism. St. Anthony and his followers started as a community of hermits, devoted to prayer, simplicity of life, celibacy, and asceticism. As time passed the lives of the monks became more organized and communal. Eventually, the eastern monasteries adopted the Rule of St. Basil.

Eastern monks have been and remain powerful spiritual forces. Since Eastern bishops are required to be celibate, while Eastern priests may marry, the bishops are generally chosen from among the monks.

Ecclesiastic

A word that comes from the Latin for "church," the term *ecclesiastic* refers to people holding Church office, such as a bishop or a priest. Matters having a Church reference are called ecclesiastical. Sometimes the term ecclesial is used instead.

Ecclesiology

Since the publication of Vatican II's landmark constitution on the Church, *Lumen Gentium,* there has been significant reflection on the meaning, structure, and purpose of the Church. The theological discipline that explores this development is ecclesiology.

Economy of Salvation

Because the term *economy* is so firmly associated with financial matters, it can be misleading when applied to salvation. The Greek origin of the term speaks of stewardship or of managing a household. It entered religious language as a way of describing God's wise creation and management of the world and above all the plan of salvation. This plan encompasses creation, the fall of man, the covenants with Israel, the redemption of the world by Jesus Christ, the continuance of salvation through the Church and the sacraments, the witness of the New Covenant people, and the second coming of Christ.

Ecumenical Councils

The Church has held twenty-one ecumenical (or universal) councils. These councils are gatherings of all the world's bishops, acting collegially with one another and in union with the pope. The council fathers address pastoral, doctrinal, moral, and disciplinary issues, depending on the needs of the Church in a given age.

For example, the first four councils in the fourth and fifth centuries upheld the divinity of Christ against Arian disbe-lief. The Council of Trent in the six-teenth century responded to Protestant challenges and initiated the Counter-Reformation. The Second Vatican Council developed a number of pastoral responses to issues the Church encoun-ters in the modern world. Ecumenical councils demonstrate the exercise of the Church's Magisterium in its fullest sense.

Ecumenism

In the Great Schism of 1054, the Byzantine Churches broke with Rome. In the sixteenth century the Protestant Reformation caused another major break with the Catholic Church. The ecumenical movement is designed to heal these divisions and restore the unity of all Christians.

The Vatican has established a secre-tariat for the promotion of Christian unity. Major, long-term dialogues have begun between Catholics and the Protestant and Orthodox churches. There are also formal interreligious dia-logues with Judaism, Islam, and other world religions. One significant out-come of ecumenism is the elimination of angry polemics and the adoption of respectful conversations about one another's beliefs, as well as mutual cooperation on matters of justice and charity for all. See also **Irenicism.**

Edict of Milan

In the year 313 the coemperors of the Roman Empire, Constantine and Licinius, gave freedom of religion to Christianity after centuries of persecu-tion. The edict was issued in Milan.

Eminence

The formal address for a cardinal is "Your Eminence."

Encyclical

Letters, written by popes and addressed to the whole Church and sometimes to the world itself, are called encyclicals. These pastoral letters are meant to be the most prominent forms of papal teaching other than infallible declara-tions. The encyclicals that have consis-tently drawn world attention are those devoted to social justice, world peace, and moral issues. Papal encyclicals are written to increase the understanding of the Church's doctrines and the faith of the people. The title of an encyclical is taken from the first few words of the text.

End of the World

The Church teaches that the world as we know it will come to an end. This will coincide with the second coming of Christ, who will arrive in glory to judge the living and the dead. Jesus delivered apocalyptic descriptions of the end of the world (see Mt 24:3-35). But he warned that it was futile to predict the exact day and hour for the world's end (see Mt 24:36).

However, the end of the world does not mean the obliteration of the cosmos. The book of Revelation, chapters twenty-one and twenty-two, says that our current world will be transformed into a new heaven and a new earth. This teaching is reinforced by Vatican II's pastoral declaration *The Church in the Modern World*, 39.

Enlightenment

Supported by the rise of science, the intellectuals of the eighteenth century inaugurated what has been called the Age of Reason or the Enlightenment. The emphasis on reason downplayed the legitimacy of faith and the reality of the supernatural. Talk of enlightenment implied that religion had kept people in superstitious darkness, but now they could be liberated by reason and science. On the positive side, the science-related application of reason has brought many medical benefits and human conveniences to the world.

The Enlightenment's challenge to the Church has resulted in her discovering within the truths of revelation deeper understandings of religious freedom, further refinements of the relationship of faith and reason, and greater insights into social concerns and human dignity. Meanwhile, the Church has presented forceful alternatives to the narrow secularity and spiritual impoverishment that is the contemporary outcome of the Enlightenment.

Epiclesis

At Mass in the Roman rite, just before the consecration, the priest places his folded hands over the bread and wine and prays that God will send the Holy Spirit to change these elements into Christ's Body and Blood. The epiclesis ("invocation upon") highlights the divine action needed to make the Eucharistic presence possible through the ministry of the priest.

Epiphany

The liturgical feast of Epiphany (or "manifestation") celebrates the adoration of the infant Jesus by the Magi, the Baptism of Christ at the Jordan, and the revelation of his glory at the marriage feast of Cana. Christ is manifested as Messiah to the world through the Magi, as Son of God at the Jordan baptism, and as divine Savior at Cana.

Episcopacy

The general name for the body of bishops is episcopacy, derived from the Greek word meaning "overseer."

Epistle

The letters of the New Testament include the epistles of Saints Paul, Peter,

John, James, and Jude, and those written to Saints Timothy, Titus, and Philemon and to the Hebrews. The epistles are pastoral reflections on doctrinal and moral issues that respond to questions raised or to the need for deeper understandings of the gospel message.

Eschatology

From the Greek meaning "the end," eschatology embraces teachings about the final age of salvation—the era of the Church (the "end time")—and the end *of* time itself. In a very real sense the kingdom of Christ has begun to be experienced on earth in the Spirit's living action in the Church and her members as well as in Christ's vital activity in the sacraments. Spiritual writers speak of this as "eternity touching time"; theologians often call it "realized eschatology."

Eschatology applies to the events known as the last things: death, judgment, purgatory, heaven, and hell, along with the transformation of the world into a new heaven and a new earth.

Essenes

A community of intensely spiritual Jews, known as Essenes ("the pious ones"), built a monastery for its members at Qumran by the shores of the Dead Sea. Many also lived in the nearby caves.

Some members married, while others practiced celibacy.

The Essenes began about a century before Christ and were still in existence at the time of his ministry. They emphasized the final days of the old dispensation as foretold by the prophets, when there would be a battle between the sons of light (themselves) and the sons of darkness. Penitential practices were needed and were symbolized by frequent water purifications or baptisms.

The ancient writers Pliny, Philo, and Josephus referred to the Essenes, but the best descriptions of their beliefs and lives are to be found in the Dead Sea Scrolls, discovered in 1947. Their community of about four thousand members was destroyed by the Roman troops of Vespasian in A.D. 68, but the survival of their library has been remarkably valuable for Scripture studies. The Essenes' general influence on apocalyptic expectations at the time of Christ can be demonstrated. See also **Dead Sea Scrolls**.

Eternity

People on earth live in time. God lives in eternity, as do the angels and saints. For the time-bound it is difficult to imagine eternity. But Scripture speaks of God's eternal life and love, especially seen in St. John's Gospel.

The human intuition that life will not be snuffed out at death is an indication that the seed of eternity lies quietly in everyone. Moreover, the human sense that love is greater than death provides another entry into what eternity is about. Catholic faith teaches that eternal life is received already on earth through baptism and above all in the Eucharist. Prayer, contemplation, and constant contact with the Eucharist are ways in which people gradually come to appreciate and experience, by faith, what eternity and eternal life are like.

Ethics

The philosophy that deals with what is right and wrong, good and bad, true and false, is called ethics. It is the exploration of what is moral and immoral. Ethics deals with means and ends, the acts that foster the growth of human character, and the meaning and purpose of life.

Ethics can and should be an essential partner of the Church's moral theology, which deals with God's authorship of human nature and the natural law, the divine will for human fulfillment and happiness, and the saving work of Christ freeing us from the slavery of sin that impedes the progress of the moral life. Both ethics and Christian moral teaching require a communion with truth whose author is God.

Pope John Paul II's encyclical *Veritatis Splendor* (*The Splendor of Truth*) analyzes the sources of moral thinking and behavior, how it ministers to the authentic hungers of the human heart, and how it leads to true happiness. Part Three of the *Catechism* presents a clear teaching of how a graced covenant with God, aided by the active presence of the Spirit, gives us a vision of the moral life that is satisfying and fulfilling. See also **Natural Law**.

Eucharist

In the Eucharist is found the whole treasure of the Church that is Jesus Christ. The Eucharist is the source and summit of the Christian life. At the Mass, the Eucharist makes present the saving graces of the sacrifice of Jesus on the cross and his resurrection from the dead. In the same Mass, the Eucharist is the sacred banquet, the holy meal, which at Communion feeds the participants with Christ. In the tabernacle, Christ's real presence in the Eucharist is reverenced, adored, and praised, as well as made available for the sick.

The sixth chapter of St. John's Gospel presents the most vivid teaching that the bread and wine become Christ's Body and Blood. Jesus instituted the Eucharist at the Last Supper (see Mt 26:26-28; Mk 14:22-24; Lk 22:17-20; 1 Cor 11:23-25). The Church teaches that in the Eucharist we have the Body, Blood, Soul, and Divinity of Jesus Christ. This presence comes about by the power of the Spirit, through the words and acts of the priest at Mass. The texts of the liturgy of Corpus Christi offer prayerful and faith-filled teachings on the meaning of the Eucharist.

Eulogy

At a funeral liturgy, after the Communion prayer, it is often customary for a relative or friend to give a brief eulogy (literally, a "good word") about the deceased.

Euthanasia

From the Greek word meaning "good death," euthanasia is an act that purposely brings about the death of an ailing, disabled, or dying person. It is sometimes called "mercy killing." Another version of this act is physician-assisted suicide.

Euthanasia is contrary to the law of God, who alone has authority over life and death. It is immoral and should be illegal. The Church's consistent life ethic defends life from womb to tomb.

At the same time, the Church teaches that extraordinary means to keep someone alive are not necessary. Even when death is imminent the sick should still receive ordinary, loving care. The use of painkillers to ease suffering, even at risk of shortening the sufferer's life, is acceptable so long as death is not willed but accepted as inevitable. Palliative care should be encouraged (see *Catechism,* par. 2277).

Evangelical Counsels

Poverty, chastity, and obedience, promised in the vows taken by members of religious orders and congregations, are the evangelical counsels. They are the hallmarks of the consecrated life and constitute powerful forms of identity with Christ who was poor, chaste, and obedient to his Father's will.

Evangelist

Saints Matthew, Mark, Luke, and John are called evangelists because they each authored a Gospel—in Greek, *evangelium,* a word that means "good news."

Evangelium Vitae

In his encyclical *Evangelium Vitae* (*The Gospel of Life*), Pope John Paul II mounts a critique of the culture of death in modern societies. He writes unambiguously against the social and legal approval of abortion, infanticide, and euthanasia. He narrows the possibility of capital punishment to rare cases in which a society has no other way to protect itself.

The pope points out that making evil acts legal is a perverse use of human freedom and should be resisted. He places the Church as a defender of human life from conception until natural death. By issuing the encyclical on the feast of the Annunciation, which celebrates Mary's welcoming of the Son of God who took flesh in her womb, the pope takes up the cause of the great multitude of weak and defenseless human beings, especially the unborn and those at the end of life. He insists that people should begin building a civilization of love that cherishes human life and dignity, a task that will create a culture of life.

Evangelization

With the publishing of Paul VI's encyclical *On Evangelization in the Modern World* and Pope John Paul II's encyclical *The Mission of the Redeemer*, the Church is being called to a new commitment to evangelization. This mission of the Church to bring the gospel to all peoples traces itself back to Christ's "Great Commission" to his followers to evangelize the world (see Mt 28:18-20). Evangelization energizes the participants, for it is in giving faith that we receive faith. Evangelization today is the mission of every Catholic, performed by witnessing to the gospel, entering into a dialogue of love with others, and inculturating the gospel by taking what is best in our cultures and sanctifying the rest.

Eve

The creation story in Genesis 1:29 says that Eve is the first woman, the wife of Adam.

Evil

The absence of goodness is evil. There are two kinds of evil, physical and moral. Regarding physical evil, St. Thomas Aquinas teaches that God's wisdom created a world that is journeying toward perfection. In this process, beings appear and disappear. The constructive and destructive aspects of nature coexist. Physical good and physical evil stand side by side until creation reaches perfection (see St. Thomas Aquinas, *Summa Contra Gentiles*, III, 71).

Moral evil, on the other hand, results from the free choice of angels and people. God permits moral evil because he wants to respect the freedom of his creatures and is able to draw good from it (see *Catechism*, par. 311).

God's entire response to the problem of evil is found in the saving life, message, death, and resurrection of Jesus Christ, Savior of the world (see *Catechism*, par. 309, 385). The issue of evil is best understood and overcome by fixing the eyes of faith on Christ alone, who has conquered evil.

Evolution

The process by which present organisms have developed from earlier forms by a process of natural selection and hereditary influences is the general understanding of the biological notion of evolution. The explanation of this process given by Charles Darwin and Alfred Russell Wallace in 1858 is the most influential.

The various theories of evolution do not imperil the Catholic understanding of the doctrine of creation. This doctrine states that God has brought all things into existence. God not only initiated the process of creation but providentially is present to its unfolding.

St. Augustine taught the symbolic nature of the Genesis creation story and argued that God placed *rationes seminales* (rational seeds) at the beginning, from which flowered the world as we have come to know it. Catholics may accept the view that material conditions made possible the emergence of human beings so long as it is acknowledged that God immediately creates the human soul in each one (see *Catechism,* par. 366).

Ex Cathedra

See **Infallibility**.

Examination of Conscience

It has been said that the unexamined life is not worth living. Conversely, the examined life is necessary for human and spiritual maturity. The Catholic practice of examination of conscience is linked to preparing for the sacrament of reconciliation.

Guidance for this examination may be found in one's fidelity to Christ's commandments to love God and neighbor as well as the Ten Commandments given by God to Moses. Spiritual writers also suggest examining one's predominant moral weaknesses for evidence of how well one has succeeded or failed to overcome them. While such an examination is proper prior to the sacrament, it ought to be a regular part of one's life, an accompaniment to the spiritual journey. It should not just be about one's sins, but also about the state of the soul's progress in virtues as manifested in one's thoughts, words, deeds, and attitudes.

Excommunication

To declare someone excommunicated is to say that this person is excluded from communion with the Church. The person is not only forbidden to take Holy Communion but is also deprived of the spiritual benefits that may come to the Church's members. Persons are excommunicated for certain grave sins and crimes against the Catholic religion.

Repentance and fulfillment of certain conditions can cause the excommunication to be revoked. In danger of death, an excommunicated person may be absolved by any priest so long as conversion of heart and repentance are present.

Exegesis

From the Greek word for "bringing out," exegesis is the tool used by Scripture scholars to determine the literal meaning of a text. They do this by their knowledge of the biblical languages, literary forms, cultural background, comparative texts, the analogy of faith, and the context of Scripture itself. Archaeological discoveries within the last two centuries have been useful in this task.

Exercises, Spiritual

Over four centuries ago, St. Ignatius of Loyola developed a masterful series of meditations and ascetical actions for bringing a person more deeply into the process of spiritual growth and conversion. Normally, it takes thirty days for a person to experience the exercises with the guidance of a practiced director. In four stages the person is taken through an examination of sinfulness, the rule of Christ, the passion of Christ and the resurrection of Christ.

These exercises have proven to be one of the most effective helps to spirituality ever created. The thirty-day retreat, during which the person journeys through the exercises, is alive and well today. Generally, it is sponsored by qualified directors from the Jesuit Order.

Exodus

The primordial religious experience of the Israelites was the Exodus event, which forged their identity as God's people (see the biblical books of Exodus and Joshua). The Jewish people had been reduced to slavery in Egypt and deprived of even the time to worship God. Called by God, Moses emerged as their leader. He confronted the Pharaoh with their need to worship.

Despite the subsequent plagues sent by God as chastisement, Pharaoh stubbornly refused. After the tenth plague, which caused the death of the firstborn of the Egyptians, the people were allowed to depart. They came to the Red Sea, only to find that Pharaoh and his army came to re-enslave them.

God told Moses to raise his hands over the sea, which miraculously parted. Israel marched across to freedom. The sea returned to its boundaries and drowned the Egyptian soldiers.

Israel then began a pilgrimage through the desert. God fed them with manna and quail and gave them water from the rock. At Sinai, God confirmed his covenant with them and gave them the Ten Commandments. Eventually, under Joshua, they entered the Promised Land. All these wondrous events of salvation constitute what is called the Exodus.

Exorcism

The act of releasing a person from being possessed by the devil is called exorcism. A simple prayer of exorcism is also said by the priest over someone about to be baptized to deliver the person from the power of evil. A major exorcism of a possessed person can be performed only by a priest with the permission of the bishop. The process should be carefully and prudently undertaken. See also **Diabolical Possession**.

Expiation

Sin and sacrilege introduce disorder into the world and people's souls. It is fitting and needed to perform acts that restore the order that was disturbed. Expiation accomplishes this restoration.

At every confession the penitent is given a small penance as a symbol of the need to make satisfaction for sins committed. On the cross, Jesus made an ultimate expiation for all sins. Our acts of expiation flow from his and receive their effectiveness as a result.

Exposition of the Blessed Sacrament

To increase faith in the real presence of Jesus in the Eucharist as well as to foster praise and adoration of the Blessed Sacrament, Catholic parishes often practice the Exposition of the Blessed Sacrament. A large Host is taken from the tabernacle and placed in a receptacle called a monstrance, where all can see it. This is often done during a "holy hour" of meditation and prayer.

Many parishes have introduced longer periods of exposition and adoration, including perpetual (twenty-four-hour) adoration, when sufficient numbers and fervor allow it. The devotion is an excellent support for the growth of meditative prayer and contemplation for countless numbers of people.

Extreme Unction

See **Anointing of the Sick**.

F

Faith

The response to God's revelation of his inner life and plan for salvation is faith. This faith is personal ("I believe") and communal ("We believe"). It calls for a surrender to God within the context of the community of the Church. It is a gift from God and always requires grace for its beginning and continuance.

At the same time, faith is free. God proposes what should be believed and never imposes belief upon us. Faith includes belief in the message of God's truth as found in Apostolic Tradition, Scripture, the creeds of the Church, the decrees of ecumenical councils, and the ongoing teachings of the Magisterium.

One of Scripture's greatest passages about faith may be found in Hebrews chapter eleven. Abraham is the father of faith (see Heb 11:11–12). Mary is the mother of faith.

Faithful, The Lay

By the sacrament of baptism the lay faithful (or laity) are initiated into full communion with the Church with all the graces, blessings, and responsibilities this entails. God calls the lay faithful to holiness. The term *lay faithful* applies to all members of the Church except those in holy orders and members of religious orders and congregations. See also **Laity**.

Fall of Man

Genesis chapter three describes the reality of sin in human history as a fall from grace. Pictured in figurative language, the story of the Fall affirms a primordial event that indeed took place at the beginning of human history. With the certainty of faith, divine revelation tells us that all of human history is affected by the original sin of our first parents (see *Catechism,* par. 388, 390).

This event should always be balanced by the good news of salvation brought to us by Christ. Connected to the disobedient choice of our first parents is the voice of the tempter, Satan, one of the fallen angels who rebelled against God (see *Catechism,* par. 391-95). See also **Devil; Sin, Original**.

Familiaris Consortio

This is an apostolic exhortation written by Pope John Paul II on the state of marriage and the family in the modern world. The pope explores both the shadows and the bright spots of the current state of the family, including a family "Bill of Rights" (see *Familiaris Consortio,* 46).

Fasting

Rooted in Scripture and Church history, the practice of fasting is a spiritual discipline meant to purify the soul and open one to God's will. Jesus fasted forty days in the desert to prepare for his messianic ministry (see Lk 4:1-2). Adult Catholics are expected to fast on Ash Wednesday and Good Friday. This means eating no more than one full meal on those days and eating lightly at the other two. Voluntary fasting at other times is recommended, according to one's health and other circumstances, and with the guidance of a spiritual director. See also **Abstinence**.

Father, God the

Scripture gradually reveals the inner life of God. When Moses experienced God at the burning bush, he heard that God's name was personal: "I AM." God is an "I."

Moses thus learned that God was not impersonal like the gods of the pagans who worshiped stars, sun, and moon. As a result, God's people came to know him as one who thought of them with love and care. God was not some thing, but some One.

In Jesus it became clear that God is our Father. God is Father in relationship to his only Son. The Son is only Son in relation to his Father. Because of Jesus we are adopted sons and daughters of God the Father.

When Jesus taught us to pray, he invited us to begin by saying, "Our Father." This is why we pray in the creed, "I believe in God, the Father almighty."

Fathers of the Church

When public revelation came to an end with the last of the scriptural writings, the understanding of revelation had to continue. This was prompted by the pastoral need both to nourish people's faith and to respond to objections to the faith. The first centuries of Christianity thus yielded outstanding pastoral teachers, known as fathers of the Church.

The fathers include men from the East such as St. Basil, St. John Chrysostom, and St. Athanasius; and men from the West such as St. Augustine, St. Ambrose, and St. Jerome. Their sermons and writings were models and benchmarks of how to make the truths of revelation disclose their hidden depths for the purposes of spiritual growth and defense against false interpretation. Their special genius was to keep scholarship and pastoral concern united.

Fear of God

One of the seven gifts of the Holy Spirit, the fear of God means that people should fear to sin so as not to be separated from the love of Christ.

Biblical fear is related to the sense of awe and reverence that results from an authentic experience of God. Scriptural fear honors the majesty of God and the mystery of his otherness.

This fear differs from being merely scared or frightened. In Scripture, nearly all appearances of God or heavenly beings are accompanied by the words, "Do not be afraid." Love is better than terror. St. John writes that love gets rid of this kind of fear (see 1 Jn 4:18).

Feasts of the Church

Liturgical feasts properly refer to celebrations of the mysteries of Christ, especially Christmas, Epiphany, Good Friday, and Easter. Other feast days, especially of Mary and the other saints, show us how the redemption of Christ has worked wonders of holiness in the lives of these models and intercessors.

Filioque

The Nicene Creed, recited each Sunday, contains the words of faith that the Holy Spirit proceeds from the Father "and the Son" (Latin *filioque;* see *Catechism,* par. 246).

Fire, Blessing of

The Easter Vigil begins with the lighting and blessing of the new fire. The rising of fire from the inert wood symbolizes the rising of Jesus from the dead. As all the candles, held by the worshipers, are lit from the original fire, the symbolism broadens to mean that the risen Christ is the light of the world. In addition, since heat is necessary for life, the new fire points to Christ as the life of the believers. This reality is dramatized by the reception of converts into full communion in the sacraments of initiation.

First Friday Devotion

Christ appeared several times to St. Margaret Mary Alacoque in the seventeenth century and asked her to promote devotion to his Sacred Heart. The devotion would entail going to Mass and Communion for nine consecutive first Fridays of the month. People faithful to this practice would receive the grace of final perseverance in the faith.

Christ's revelations of his love countered the prevailing Jansenism of the time, which emphasized guilt and fear and curtailed frequent reception of the Eucharist. The focus on God's love was a welcome change and created a more wholesome and balanced faith. This form of popular devotion has nurtured the faith of millions and is still practiced by many.

First Holy Communion

The first time one goes to Holy Communion is rightly celebrated with special ceremony. This is particularly true in the case of children. Today a child of seven may be admitted to Communion.

A decree of Pope St. Pius X in 1910 said that children who have reached the "age of reason or discretion" may receive Communion. This means that the child should be able to know and believe that the consecrated host is really Christ's Body. Pope Pius wanted to promote frequent reception of the Eucharist in a time when the practice was not common.

Children and adults are prepared for first Communion by a catechesis that explains the meaning and purpose of the sacrament. Children are expected also to have had a catechesis for their first confession and be admitted to that sacrament before they make their first Communion. Frequently the girls wear white dresses and the boys wear white suits for their first Communion; other rituals are also used to make the occasion memorable.

First Saturday Devotion

At Fatima, Mary was said to have recommended this devotion, which was started by St. John Eudes in the seventeenth century. It involves attending Mass and receiving Communion on five consecutive first Saturdays of the month; confession either before or after the series; the recitation of the Rosary; and a fifteen-minute meditation on one of the mysteries. Perseverance in faith at the hour of death is promised.

Focolare

Chiara Lubich began the Focolare movement in Italy in 1943. It promotes a spirituality based on Christ's prayer that all may be one. This search for unity through prayer, spirituality, and practical love has proved popular and effective. Centers for the movement exist in sixty countries.

Form Criticism

A method used by Scripture scholars, form criticism is a painstaking effort to trace the history of how individual textual units within the Gospels developed from the oral stage to their present written forms. This would include estimating how the units were understood and shaped along the way.

Fornication

It is God's will that sexual relations should be confined to the bonds of marriage. Fornication is a sexual act between an unmarried male and female. The act is contrary to the sixth commandment.

Fortitude

One of the four cardinal moral virtues, fortitude is an attitude and an act that keeps a person firmly focused on God's will when tempted to sin. Like any virtue, fortitude is the result of repeated practice, prayer, the example and inspiration of other morally courageous people, and the grace of the Holy Spirit. It is one of the seven gifts of the Spirit.

Forty Hours Devotion

Faith in the real presence of Christ in the Eucharist always needs some kind of renewal. Whenever a crisis of faith arises in this area, the Holy Spirit prompts the Church to respond. The Reformation introduced such a crisis of faith regarding the Eucharist. A divine response came through saints such as Philip Neri of Rome and Charles Borromeo of Milan, who supported the growth of the new Forty Hours Devotion, recalling the forty hours Jesus spent in the tomb.

The devotion includes forty hours of (semi) continuous adoration of the Blessed Sacrament exposed in a monstrance for the adoration of the people. This exposition is accompanied by Masses, a procession, and sermons that illumine the mystery of the Eucharist. Most parishes have modified forms of this devotion today.

Franciscans

In the thirteenth century, St. Francis of Assisi underwent a conversion from a rich man's son to a practitioner of evangelical poverty. The number of his followers grew to the point that they needed organization into what became the Franciscan Order. St. Clare of Assisi founded a female version in her contemplative Poor Clare Order.

Numerous other congregations of active Franciscan sisters were eventually established. A later reform of the men's order resulted in the Franciscan Capuchins. Taken together, all the variations of Franciscans, men and women, form the largest community of consecrated life in the Church. St. Francis is perhaps the Church's most popular saint, even widely admired by many non-Catholics.

Freedom

All people are created in the image and likeness of God. One essential aspect of this image is the capacity to be free. How is one to handle this precious gift of freedom?

St. Anselm teaches that every time people sin, their freedom is diminished. Every time people perform a good act, the capacity to be free increases. Hence freedom's best hope is virtue.

The more we sin, the less we are free. The more we do God's will, the greater freedom we possess. Behavioral sciences point out that psychological anxieties and social pressures affect the exercise of freedom. Hence it would seem that a healthy psyche as well as a wholesome soul are conditions for achieving the goal of ever-liberating freedom.

Therapy for the behaviorally disabled is one step. Grace and spirituality is a concomitant other step on the road to freedom. See also **Liberty, Religious.**

Fruits of the Holy Spirit

The Holy Spirit endows the responsive soul with twelve fruits of his creative action. They are the first signs of the impact of eternal glory on our temporal lives. The list is found in the *Catechism*, par. 1832.

Fundamental Option

Pope John Paul II, in his encyclical *Veritatis Splendor* (*The Splendor of Truth*), writes that people make a fundamental option for or against God. This is a conscious and deliberate choice, not a subconscious one. People know what they are doing.

Individual moral or immoral acts affect the quality of the choice. Venial sin weakens the choice. Mortal sin, which deprives one of the state of grace until the person repents and seeks forgiveness, weakens the option even more. Still the option for God remains, so long as it is not deliberately revoked.

The pope rejects a view of the fundamental option that states the choice is subconscious, that moral acts do not affect it, and that there is no mortal sin. The pope finds this a pastorally deficient position. Instead, he encourages the faithful to strengthen their fundamental option by acts that support a joyful surrender to God. He calls people to prayer, openness to the graces of the sacraments, a deeper, personal union with Jesus, and commitment to Christian morality.

Funeral Liturgy

At the Mass of Christian Burial, the casket is covered with a white cloth to remind everyone of the white robe the person received at baptism. The paschal candle is lit to recall the candle given to the newly baptized, symbolizing that the risen Christ is their light of salvation and the divine life of the soul. The deceased person is surrounded with memories of the first sacraments received that launched him or her on the journey of faith.

The theme of the Mass is that life is changed, not taken away. The mystery of Christ's death is present in the sacrificial character of the Eucharist. The sadness of losing a loved one here is acknowledged and the grieving of the mourners is united to Christ's passion. The mourners' hope of eternal life and the resurrection of the body for their loved one is united to Christ's resurrected triumph over death. A Catholic funeral embraces the tears of sorrow and of joy simultaneously: grief for the loss, joy for the hope. Faith pervades the entire liturgical experience.

G

Gabriel

The name of one of the seven archangels, Gabriel means "man of God" or "God has shown himself mighty." Gabriel appeared to the prophet Daniel to explain a vision Daniel had received (see Dn 8:15ff; 9:21ff).

In St. Luke's Gospel, Gabriel appeared to St. Zechariah to tell him that his aged wife, St. Elizabeth, would bear a son, St. John the Baptist (see Lk 1:5-20). Six months later, Gabriel came to Mary and announced that she would bear a son conceived by the Holy Spirit (Lk 1:26-38). By his angelic messenger Gabriel, God gradually prepared the world for the revelation of his only Son, who would be Messiah and Savior for the world.

Gabriel is the "power" angel inasmuch as he reveals how God's power would change the world and provide the means for a victory over evil.

Galilee

Jesus was raised in Galilee, the northern part of the Holy Land. According to the Gospels of St. Matthew, St. Mark, and St. Luke, it was in Galilee that he exercised the first part of his messianic ministry. This was the springtime of his mission because he was so well received at first.

Galilee borders the sea that bears its name. Jesus made the seaside town of Capernaum his headquarters during the Galilean ministry. The territory is the site of well-known cities referred to in the Gospels such as Nazareth, Tiberias, Magdala, and Bethsaida. Mount Tabor and the Valley of Esdraelon are in the southern part of Galilee. All the apostles came from Galilee.

Gaudium et Spes

This is a document of Vatican II that explores the pastoral role of the Church in the modern world. As the last of the council documents, it contains exhortations to contemplate and implement the whole work of the council. In a special way its pastoral tone complements the document on the Church (*Lumen Gentium*), which was more theological in character.

Another characteristic of the document is its affinity with the social teachings of the Church, advising the faithful to read the signs of the times in the light of the Gospel. Related to this is the emphasis on human dignity, noting that Jesus Christ reveals to us what is genuinely human about us (n. 22). Its closing statement is often quoted: "Let there be unity in what is necessary, freedom in what is doubtful, and charity in everything" (n. 92).

General Confession and Absolution

This is a communal form of the sacrament of reconciliation. It is only permitted in cases of grave need when there is no time for individual confessions nor a sufficient number of priests to hear them, such as during wartime when a battle is imminent. The penitents quietly express sorrow for all their sins and resolve in due time to confess grave sins that cannot be confessed at present. Prayers are said. Then a general absolution is given to the penitents. The diocesan bishop determines when this may be done within his diocese.

Genocide

The deliberate killing of innocent populations because of their ethnic, religious, or national identity is genocide. For example, in the death camps of World War II millions of Jews, other ethnic groups, and thousands of priests were murdered. Recent attempts at ethnic cleansing in the Balkans are another example. The methodical extermination of a race, nation, or ethnic minority is a crime against humanity deserving condemnation.

Gentile

Jewish people in Old Testament times referred to members of other nations as *goyim*. The term was translated as "Gentiles" in New Testament times and has remained a description for non-Jews.

Genuflection

The bending of one knee to the floor and rising again is a genuflection and an act of reverence for the Blessed Sacrament. A genuflection is normally done before one enters a pew at church and upon departure from the church. The priest celebrant at Mass genuflects several times, such as after the showing of the Eucharistic bread and the chalice, and again before the Communion.

Gifts of the Holy Spirit

Traditionally the Holy Spirit is honored for seven gifts to us: wisdom, understanding, knowledge, courage, counsel, piety, and fear of the Lord. The list is derived from Isaiah 11:1-3. These gifts belong in their fullness to Christ. The Holy Spirit fills us with these gifts so that we are disposed to obey his divine promptings (see Rom 8:14, 17).

Gift of Tongues

Speaking in tongues is a gift of the Holy Spirit. It means ecstatic speech in a language not understood by the speaker or the listeners. St. Paul teaches that it is a gift of the Spirit that is meant to build up the faith of the Church. Because of its mysterious nature, it requires a Spirit-led interpreter. Read all of chapter fourteen of Corinthians for St. Paul's pastoral approach to the use of this gift.

Glorified Body

The risen Christ appeared in his glorified body. The Easter narratives point out that this body could be seen, touched, and recognized. Christ, risen, could eat a meal. He retained the scars of his passion. At the same time, his body had unusual qualities, such as the ability to appear and disappear at will, as well as to pass through closed doors. This glorified body is incorruptible.

In heaven our bodies will be like Christ's. St. Paul devotes a lengthy explanation to what our glorified bodies will be like, building on the comparison of a wheat seed that dies and corrupts, but rises a sheaf of wheat (see 1 Cor 15:35-58). Still, this is a religious mystery that exceeds our imagination and understanding and is accessible only by faith.

Glory

The Old Testament uses the images of a radiant cloud and a pillar of fire to describe the experience of God's presence. The words for the cloud and the fire are *shekinah* and *kabod*. They mean "glory" and refer to the gracious appearance of the Lord.

God is utter mystery and dwells in deep darkness as far as our ability to see him. But God also wants to reach us and share himself with us. The glory appearances in the Old Testament—as at the burning bush and Sinai—prefigured the magnificent appearance of the Son of God in Jesus Christ.

St. John's Gospel picks up the theme of the glory from the Old Testament and applies it frequently to Christ. St. John writes that glory is a name for Christ's divinity. Christ's miracle at Cana is the first time he reveals his glory-divinity (see Jn 2:1-11). The book of Revelation is filled with scenes of glory, radiating from the heavenly throne room into the worship of the early Christians at liturgy. In heaven we will be embraced by the glory that will be our source of eternal joy.

Glory Be to the Father

These are the first words of a frequently used prayer: "Glory be to the Father, and to the Son, and to the Holy Spirit. As it was in the beginning, is now and ever shall be, world without end, Amen." It is said after each psalm in the Liturgy of the Hours and after each decade of the Rosary.

Gluttony

One of the seven capital sins, gluttony refers to the unrestrained appetite for food and drink.

God

The creator of heaven and earth, angels and humans, God is the providential and saving Presence to the cosmos and humans. God is a Trinity of Father, Son, and Spirit in loving communion with one another. While all three Persons always act in harmony toward creation, each Person is seen as having a special love for us: the Father as Creator and Provider, the Son as Redeemer, the Holy Spirit as Sanctifier.

When the doctrine of the Trinity was being undermined by objections, the early councils of the Church responded with an explanation based on the notions of "person" and "substance." "The Church uses the term 'substance' (rendered also at times by 'essence' or 'nature') to designate the divine being in its unity" (*Catechism*, par. 252). Each Person is God whole and entire.

Despite the mystery surrounding God, we have God's Son, Jesus Christ, who revealed a great deal about who God is and what he is like. St. John summed God up in a limpid, simple description: "God is love" (1 Jn 4:8). See also **Incarnation; Nicaea; Trinity**.

Godparents

A godfather and godmother serve as sponsors and helpers for the newly baptized—child or adult—on the road to the Christian life. Obviously parents bear the primary responsibility for the faith growth of a child. Godparents, who should be practicing Catholics, are essential supporters of this important goal. A non-Catholic Christian, together with a godparent, may serve as a witness to a baptism, but not as a godparent. Ultimately the whole community of believers needs to safeguard the graces given at baptism.

Golgotha

Another name for Calvary, the site of Christ's crucifixion, Golgotha means "the place of the skull."

Good Friday

Jesus Christ was crucified on a Friday called "good" because it was the day we were saved from the tyranny of sin and death. Jesus had taught that there is no greater love than to lay down one's life out of love for another (see Jn 15:13). God could find no greater way to prove his care for us than to die for love of us.

Goodness

As images of God, we have been given a will with the capacity to love the good. This gift of choice holds within it the greatest potential for happiness. Each time we choose the good, the happier we become, even when the good entails sacrifice and pain.

Goodness is creative, the very opposite of evil, which causes self-destruction and death. The creative potential of goodness identifies us more closely with God each time a good act is performed. God is pure goodness.

St. Thomas Aquinas revealed the connection of goodness with beauty, truth, and unity. The more we are filled with goodness, the more we become beautiful, true, and united to God, other people, and all creation.

Gospels

The word *gospel* means "good news." The four Gospels, written by Saints Matthew, Mark, Luke, and John, have proven to be the most powerful books of Scripture in the Church's work of evangelization. The Gospels place Jesus Christ at the center, proclaiming his person, message, kingdom, and salvation. They call the listeners and readers to faith, baptism, and membership in the kingdom community that is the Church.

Each Gospel was originally addressed to a specific audience but now speaks to all the world. The individual Gospels give unique pictures of Jesus. For example, St. Matthew shows us Christ as a new Moses, the Lawgiver of the New Covenant. St. Mark pictures Christ as the Jesus of the cross. In St. Luke we encounter the Jesus of prayer, compassion, forgiveness, and sensitivity to women's needs. In St. John, we stand in awe before the divine Presence in Jesus, whose risen life shines over the whole text. To obtain the full and rounded portrait of Jesus, we must take into account all four Gospels.

The Gospels are the heart of Scripture. All of the Old Testament leads up to the Gospels. All of the other New Testament books unfold the majesty and meaning of the Gospels.

Grace

Derived from the Latin word for "gift," grace reflects the loving plan by which Father, Son, and Spirit sought to save us and bring us divine life. This is a free and undeserved gift that makes us adopted sons and daughters of God. Grace is the action of the Holy Spirit in the sacraments and in our souls.

Grace is another name for divine love and divine life. The theology of grace tells us of the help we receive from God to allow the process of salvation to be effective in our lives. Grace is also the very life of God dwelling in our hearts (see *Catechism*, par. 1996-2003).

Grace at Meals

The traditional blessing prayer of grace at a meal is this: "Bless us, O Lord, and these your gifts, which we have received from your goodness through Christ our Lord, Amen." Spontaneous meal prayers are often said and formal, composed prayers are used for special occasions.

Gregorian Chant

Named after Pope St. Gregory the Great (540–604), who compiled and arranged this ancient form of Church music, Gregorian chant has a deceptive simplicity. Its greatest strength is that it serves the biblical and liturgical words without drawing attention to itself. It is a "servant of the Word."

Unlike contemporary music, which involves accompaniment and harmony, the chant melodies work well with voices alone and do not need harmonizing. Not structured in the customary ways of contemporary music, the chant communicates a sense of peace and freedom in the ebb and flow of its progress. Chant is well suited to the spiritual and transcendent nature of worship.

After Vatican II, Gregorian chant was unfortunately laid aside in many parishes in favor of the new vernacular hymns. However, it did survive in the Our Father, where the old melody is often used with vernacular words. In some places, the chant is making a comeback. In time, it should resume a deserved and prominent place among the available forms of Church music for use in liturgy.

Grille

Cloistered communities of religious women provide a grille to separate them from family members, friends, and guests who are visiting them. Made of metal or wood, it is a grating of various designs, open enough to facilitate communication, yet still symbolizing the enclosure to which the nuns are committed. A grille is also used in confessionals where the priest and penitent are not face to face. It is tightly woven to preserve the anonymity of the penitent.

Guardian Angels

The feast of Guardian Angels on October 2 provides the context of faith and prayer about God's generosity in giving each of us an angel to look after our needs.

Habit
See **Virtue**.

Habit, Religious
The robes worn by male and female members of religious orders and congregations are known as religious habits. These distinctive forms of dress are like uniforms that identify the wearers as belonging to consecrated life in its many historic forms. The robes are called habits because they symbolize the virtues that the male and female religious have promised to acquire and live by, especially the evangelical counsels of poverty, chastity, and obedience.

Hagiography
From the Greek words *graphein* and *hagia*—meaning to "write the holy." Hagiography refers to biographies of the saints. The lives of the saints have always been popular because they inspire people to a renewal of faith and a strengthening of their commitment to Christ and the Church. The saints witness to the wondrous variety of ways in which the gospel can be lived with heroic virtue. There are saints from every walk of life: lawyers, nurses, farmers, writers, soldiers, kings, doctors, peasants, aristocrats, marrieds, singles, young and old, men and women. People hunger to know that holiness is possible. The saints illustrate that God's grace makes sanctity happen.

Hail Mary
Along with the Our Father, the Hail Mary is one of the most popular prayers in the Church. The first half of the prayer comes from a combination of the greeting Gabriel spoke to Mary at the Annunciation—"Hail, favored one! The Lord is with you" (Lk 1:28 NAB)—and the words of Elizabeth to Mary at the Visitation: "Blessed are you among women, and blessed is the fruit of your womb" (Lk 1:42). The second half may be traced to the Council of Ephesus (A.D. 431) where the bishops declared that our Blessed Mother was "Holy Mary, Mother of God" (in Greek, *Theotokos*—literally, "God bearer"). The final sentence was added as a prayer for her intercession. It has been estimated that over one billion Hail Marys are said every day, especially in the recitation of the Rosary.

Happiness
The inner, spiritual experience of cotentment and joy characterizes the happiness that all people desire. Paradoxically, happiness can coexist with suffering,

trials, and setbacks, so long as the proper inner attitudes prevail. Jesus opened his Sermon on the Mount with a reflection on happiness to be achieved by living the attitudes embodied in the eight Beatitudes.

The best way to beatitude (or happiness) is to enter into union with God and practice the various directions given by Christ's gospel teachings. God alone can satisfy the human heart completely. Perfect happiness can only be achieved in heaven. Ultimately, enduring happiness is a gift from God (see *Catechism*, par. 1716-24).

Hatred

An attitude of hostility and malevolence toward another person or group, hatred is the source of great evil in the world. The hatred of the fallen angels (Satan and devils) for God motivates them to undermine the faith of believers. Ethnic hatreds breed anger and resentments that erupt into violence, cruelty, torture, and similar behavior toward enemies. In ordinary families, hatreds flare up between the closest of relatives, resulting in lifelong animosity and alienation. When large, armed nations acquire festering hatreds, terrible destructive wars are unleashed.

Hatred destroys both the hater and the hated. How should hatred be treated? The Our Father and the whole gospel urge forgiveness as the antidote

to hatred. Scripture teaches that God is rich in mercy. We are expected to be merciful as God is merciful (see Lk 6:36). Moreover, there should be a hatred for sin and evil, but in the spirit of the axiom, "Hate the sin, not the sinner."

Heaven

The destiny of human life is final union with God in heaven, the abode of the saved. Heaven is a state of perfect happiness. In it, we will have communion with the Father, Son, and Holy Spirit; we will have communion with Mary, the other saints, and the angels; and we will join our loved ones who have preceded us there. Scripture speaks of heaven as eternal life, which is partially experienced here on earth through participation in the sacraments, the depths of prayer, and acts of unselfish love for others. While heaven is a state that no eye has seen nor ear has heard, nor can it be sufficiently described (see 1 Cor 2:9), yet it was pictured by Jesus, who used images of light, life, and wedding dinners to give us some hint of how wonderful it is.

Polls report that most people believe in some kind of heaven and expect to go there after death. This rosy view needs to be balanced by Christ's teaching that avoiding sin and staying in grace is necessary to get into heaven.

Hedonism

The view that self-gratification is the highest priority, hedonism prevails among people who substitute immediate pleasure for long-range happiness. The narcissistic person places the needs of self above any concern for others. Hedonism prizes the pleasures of sex, food, money, power, fashion, possessions, and instant gratification over any restraint or sense of deeper spiritual values.

Hedonism corrupts the person and is capable of destroying a whole culture. It is both immoral and amoral. Freedom from hedonism requires a moral and spiritual conversion.

Hell

The tragic outcome after death for people who have failed to love God or others in this life is hell. Christ's description of the Last Judgment shows God sending into eternal fire those who did not feed the hungry, clothe the naked, take care of the sick, or care for the needy in other ways (see Mt 25:41-46). As people live, so shall they die.

People who live evil lives right up to their last breath can hardly expect to be different in the next life. It is on earth that the decisions are made about eternal destiny. Hell describes the result of the decision to exclude oneself from communion with God. Such people choose not to avoid sin on earth. Committed to evil here, they will live in evil there.

Studies claim that many people believe in hell but do not believe they will go there. This is a comforting illusion for those stuck in evil. Conversion to God before death is necessary.

Heresy

When baptized people, with full knowledge and consent, deny the Church's divinely given teaching authority, they are in heresy.

Hermeneutics

From a Greek word meaning "interpretation," hermeneutics refers to the academic discipline of interpreting Scripture.

Hermit

People who choose to live the consecrated life in a solitary manner are called hermits. They give themselves to the contemplation of God in silence, prayer, and penance for the salvation of the world. Members of the Carthusian Order, for example, lead a hermitic life, but with some brief times set aside for community.

Heroic Virtue

In the canonization process, it is essential to prove that the candidate for sainthood has been a person of heroic virtue. Such candidates should have practiced the virtues of faith, hope, love, prudence, justice, temperance, and courage out of love for God and people, over an extended period of time, in an exemplary manner. Their lives of virtue are a testimonial to grace.

Hierarchy

The pope and bishops, as successors to St. Peter and the other apostles, form the hierarchy of the Church.

Hierarchy of Truths

The truths of faith are arranged in a hierarchy of importance, though all are essential for belief. This hierarchy might be imagined as a series of concentric circles, with the Holy Trinity in the center and all other doctrines related to Father, Son, and Spirit in various ways. These truths form a coherent whole and are meant to be kept harmoniously in relation to each other.

Holiness, Call to

God calls all people to holiness (see Lv 11:45). Vatican II echoes this truth in its section on the universal call to holiness (see *Lumen Gentium*, chapter 5). In a vital way this call is addressed to the members of the Church who have been blessed with the gift of faith, the graces of the sacraments, and the support of the community of believers.

The ordained members serve the sanctification of the baptized, who in turn are asked to serve the sanctification of the world. The process of becoming holy involves the resolute avoidance of sin, the practice of virtue, and openness to the power of the Holy Spirit's guidance. Bringing holiness to others implies having first acquired it for oneself. See also **Marks of the Church**.

Holocaust

One of the forms of Israelite sacrifice in which the entire victim—a lamb or a bull—was offered to God and consumed by fire (see Ex 29:38-42; Lv 6:8-10). The holocaust symbolized the ideal surrender of people of faith to God's will.

The term *holocaust* as a deed of "thorough destruction" came to be applied in modern times to the act of genocide of six million Jewish people by the Nazis. Millions of Poles, gypsies, and others were also similarly murdered. It illustrates the depth of evil that humans are capable of, as well as the need for the graces of salvation that would prevent the human soul from ever doing this again. The Jewish community has been effective in establishing holocaust memorials and other public reminders to assure that the tragedy will not be forgotten—or repeated.

Holy Days of Obligation

Important Church feasts, besides Sundays, on which Catholics are obliged to participate in the Eucharist are called holy days of obligation.

Christmas; Easter; the Solemnity of Mary, Mother of God; and the Assumption of Mary are examples of holy days that are universally observed.

Holy Family

Jesus, Mary, and Joseph are honored as the members of the Holy Family. The feast of the Holy Family is observed on the Sunday after Christmas. In a sermon about the Holy Family, Pope Paul VI commended three of its virtues: First, meditative silence reflected the religious nature of this family; second, they modeled family life as a community of love and sharing; third, the home of a carpenter illustrated a respect for work and discipline.

Holy Father

The pope is given the title Holy Father to indicate his vocation to serve the sanctification of the Church's members as well as to remain firm in his own commitment to a life of holiness.

Holy Hour

The Catholic devotion of the holy hour centers on the adoration of the Holy Eucharist exposed in a monstrance. The service includes prayers, hymns, and periods of silence, and concludes with Benediction of the Blessed Sacrament. Many Catholics make a private holy hour, devoting their time before the tabernacle to prayer and silent medita-

tion. The late Archbishop Fulton J. Sheen made a holy hour every day of his priesthood, saying that it was "the hour that made his day."

Holy of Holies

Scripture describes the Jerusalem Temple as a building surrounded by various courtyards, one for Gentiles, the other two for Jewish women and men. Jewish people did not go into the temple building to worship. Instead, sacrifices were offered on an altar in front of the temple.

The temple structure contained three holy rooms. The innermost room, shaped as a cube with no windows, was called the Holy of Holies. In Solomon's temple, the Ark of the Covenant was housed here. Once a year, on the Day of Atonement, the high priest entered the Holy of Holies and offered sacrifices.

Solomon's temple lasted four centuries. Another temple was built by King Herod the Great. This was the temple Jesus knew. It was destroyed by the Romans in A.D. 70. See also **Temple of Jerusalem**.

Holy Office

Now called the Office for the Doctrine of the Faith, this department of the Vatican supervises the purity of the Church's doctrinal and moral teachings. It examines and evaluates theological developments especially as they appear in theological books and articles. It provides clarification of Church teachings when this is deemed necessary.

This office presides over the process for handling cases of serious departure from Church doctrine by clergy or other prominent Catholic teachers. The Holy Office is directed by a cardinal. In centuries past it was known as the Holy Roman and Universal Inquisition.

Holy Oils

The rites of anointing for various sacraments require Holy Oils. These oils are blessed at a special Mass by the bishop during Holy Week. There are three kinds of oils: *Holy Chrism*, used for baptism, confirmation, and the anointing of priests' hands and the heads of bishops at ordination; *Oil of the Sick*, for the sacrament of anointing; and *Oil of Catechumens*, used for candidates before their baptism at the Rite of Christian Initiation. Holy Scripture gives many instances of using blessed oil to anoint priests, prophets, and kings.

Holy Orders

The sacrament of holy orders is administered to deacons, priests, and bishops at their respective ordinations. In this sacrament, the mission that Christ entrusted to his apostles is continued to the end of time. The term *order* is taken from the Latin *ordo*, which described an established governing body in ancient Roman society. So an ordination is an investiture into an order.

The ordained deacon, priest, and bishop receive a permanent sacramental character by which they are meant to be as devoted to Christ's covenant with the Church as he is. Along with matrimony, holy orders is a sacrament of communion, meaning that it is designed to build up the communal nature of the Church. The ordained ministerial priesthood is different in kind, not just in degree, from the common priesthood of all the lay faithful given at their baptism.

Holy Saturday

The third day of the Triduum in Holy Week, Holy Saturday rounds out the celebration of the paschal mystery at the Easter Vigil, which begins after sundown that night. See also **Vigil**.

Holy See

Coming from the Latin *sedes*, "chair," the see or seat is the center of episcopal administration. The Holy See is the administrative and spiritual center of the Catholic Church, because its head is the pope, the bishop of Rome, successor of the apostle Peter and pastor of the universal Church. While its principal offices are in and near the Vatican, the Holy See is not identified with the Vatican City State but with the diocese of

Rome, which houses the pope's cathedral at the basilica of St. John Lateran.

Holy Sepulchre

At Jerusalem in A.D. 335, the first church of the Holy Sepulchre was built over the site of Calvary and the tomb from which Jesus rose. It was erected by the emperor Constantine after the discovery of the True Cross. Persian invaders destroyed it in 614. The Crusaders built a new church in 1149. That church was ruined by a fire in 1808.

In 1810 the present church was constructed by the Greeks and Armenians. Custody of the church today is shared by the Franciscans and representatives of the Orthodox Church. Marble shrines enclose both the site of Calvary and Christ's tomb. It is one of the world's most revered shrines for all Christian believers.

Holy Spirit

The Holy Spirit is the Third Person of the Blessed Trinity. In the Nicene Creed we affirm by faith that the Holy Spirit is the Lord (God) and Giver of life, who proceeds from the Father and the Son. The Spirit is to be worshiped and glorified.

In the New Testament, the Spirit is imaged as a dove at Christ's Baptism (see Mt 3:16); as a radiant cloud at Christ's transfiguration (see Mt 17:5); by the breath of Christ on Easter night when he gave the apostles the gift of forgiving sins (see Jn 20:22); and by tongues of fire at Pentecost when the Spirit manifested the Church (Acts 2:3). The Holy Spirit abides with the Church, teaches what Christ has taught, and is the source of the constant renewal of the Church. The Spirit's power is present in all the sacraments, especially in confirmation, in which the person is sealed with the Spirit. The seven gifts of the Spirit enable the faithful to grow in grace and virtue.

Holy Thursday

The first day of the sacred Triduum of Holy Week, Holy Thursday commemorates the institution of the Holy Eucharist and the establishing of the priesthood. The Last Supper accounts of the institution of the Eucharist are found in the first three Gospels, as well as in 1 Corinthians 11:23-26. The liturgy for the day includes the washing of the feet. See also **Eucharist**.

Holy Water

Water blessed by the priest is placed in fonts at the entrance to churches. People entering the church dip their fingers in the holy water and make the sign of the cross to recall Christ's saving act as well as their own baptism. Holy water is used for all other blessings by the Church. Families may get a supply of holy water to be used at home for familial blessings.

Holy Week

The sixth week of Lent is Holy Week. It begins with Passion Sunday (or Palm Sunday) and ends with the sacred Triduum of Holy Thursday, Good Friday, and Holy Saturday, which concludes with the Easter Vigil. The full account of Christ's passion is read from a synoptic Gospel (St. Matthew, St. Mark, or St. Luke) on Sunday, and the passion according to St. John is read on Good Friday.

The week celebrates the institution of the Eucharist and the priesthood, as well as the passion, death, and resurrection of Christ. It makes present, through the Eucharist, the major events of our salvation from sin and the gift of divine life.

Holy Year

Every twenty-five years the Church announces a Holy Year in which people are called to undertake a spiritual renewal, seek reconciliations that have been deferred, forgive debts, and make pilgrimages. The pope grants plenary indulgences for pilgrimages to Rome, Jerusalem, and other shrines. The custom is based on the Jewish celebration of Jubilee years (see Lv 25:10-15).

Homily

The homily is given by a priest or deacon after the Gospel reading in the Mass. The homily explains the Scriptures that have been read and applies these texts to the lives of the listeners. The homily should prepare the worshiping community to enter more actively into the liturgy of the Eucharist that follows it, as well as to put into practice the exhortations to Christian spirituality, morality, and service.

Homosexuality

The sexual attraction to members of one's own sex, homosexual behavior is contrary to God's law, which states that sexual acts may only take place in marriage between a man and a woman. The *Catechism* (par. 2357-59) states that homosexuality is an objective disorder. It also notes that homosexuals should be treated with respect, compassion, and sensitivity. All unjust discrimination against them should be avoided.

Homosexuals are called to chastity and need to take advantage of all the spiritual means available to live according to God's will. The organization called Courage helps gays and lesbians to live chaste lives.

Hope

A theological virtue, hope is based on trust in Christ's promise of salvation and eternal happiness, and the graces needed to obtain this promise. The virtue of hope builds upon the natural human desire for happiness and fulfillment. The virtue purifies and uplifts human hope and places it in a spiritual realm where it is strengthened and directed to an eternal goal. The New Testament contains many inspiring passages about the value of hope and the helps that come from the Holy Spirit to live joyfully in the hope given by Christ (see Rom 5:5; Heb 6:18-20; Mt 10:22).

Hosanna

This Hebrew word means "Save us, we beseech you." It occurs six times in the Gospels and was used to acclaim Jesus during his entry into Jerusalem on Palm Sunday (see Jn 12:13). This prayer occurs in every Mass after the Preface and at the beginning of the Canon.

Host

The Latin origin of the word means a "victim for sacrifice." It has come to signify the Eucharistic bread, which is Christ's Body offered sacramentally in sacrifice for us.

Human Dignity

Because human beings receive souls from God and are thus made in God's image, they have an intrinsic value and dignity conferred by God, who invites all to eternal life. The Church's empha-

sis on human dignity in modern times is meant to counter the indiscriminate destruction of human life in wars, death camps, eugenic experiments, abortion, euthanasia, and other forms of killing. Human dignity is also assailed by economic exploitation of the poor and the devaluing of persons by materialism. The Church's social teachings about politics, society, economics, peace, and morality are all directed to the restoration of human dignity.

Humanae Vitae

This encyclical of Pope Paul VI, whose title means "of human life," examines marriage, the family, and the regulation of births. The pope upholds the Church's teaching about love and sexuality in marriage. He speaks against the use of artificial means of contraception, arguing that every sexual act should be open to the transmission of life. While the teaching proved to be controversial, it has been upheld by subsequent popes. See also **Natural Family Planning**.

Humanism

A view of life that concentrates on human virtues, potential, and fulfillment. Humanism proposes education, cultural and scientific pursuits, freedom, and self-determination as fundamental ways to create a prosperous and happy society. Secular humanism approaches this goal without reference to any religious or faith-driven aspects. Christian humanism argues that God, faith, and religion are essential for the true fulfillment of humanity.

Humeral Veil

A broad, rectangular silk cloth placed over the shoulders of a priest at Benediction of the Blessed Sacrament. The humeral veil is used by the priest to raise the monstrance and bless the people. See also **Benediction**.

Humility

The virtue of humility counteracts the sin of pride, which prevents a person from submitting to God's will and relating properly to other people. Humility takes away arrogance and other self-inflating attitudes that blind a person to the truth of life and God. For those on the road to spiritual maturity, humility is the first and lasting attitude that accompanies them.

Jesus asked us to imitate his humility (see Mt 11:29). He modeled humility at the Last Supper when he washed the feet of the apostles (see Jn 13:12-15). His patient endurance of the insults of the passion and the pain of the cross shows how profoundly he practiced humility (see Phil 2:8).

Hymns

Faith words poetically set to music, hymns have been part of worship since biblical times and throughout the history of the Church. Israel sang praises to God in psalms and hymns. So also did the New Testament Christians.

St. Augustine was fond of music and extolled hymns as "praying twice," since the music raised the prayer from prosaic words to heartfelt melodies of praise. There are hymns for all occasions: feasts of Jesus, Mary and the saints; weddings and funerals; Advent and Lent; Christmas and Easter; praise and petition. Congregational singing of hymns helps form a sense of community as well as sending prayers soaring to God.

Hyperdulia

While only God can be adored, there is a proper place for respecting and venerating the saints. The Church distinguishes *latria* (adoration of God) from *dulia* (veneration of saints). Because of the unique dignity of the Virgin Mary, the Mother of God and queen of angels and saints, the veneration due her is called *hyperdulia*.

Hypostatic Union

From the Greek *hypostasis*, meaning "person," this term refers to the role of the Son of God in uniting in his divine Person a human nature and a divine nature.

Hyssop

A spongelike branch used to sprinkle
fluids, hyssop was employed in the Old
Testament to splash sacrificial blood on
the altar. During the crucifixion, a hyssop sponge, soaked in wine, was offered
to Christ (see Mt 27:48). At the Easter
Vigil, the priest sprinkles the newly
blessed water on the congregation, usually with a metal sprinkler, but sometimes with a branch of fir or similar
plant.

I

Icon

The principle form of sacred art in the Eastern Churches, the icon, a painting on wood, is a prayerful, even mystical, representation of Christ, Mary, the other saints, or the angels. Those who are trained to do icons undergo both a rigorous apprenticeship in the art form and an intense spiritual formation.

Unlike portraits in Western art, the icon is two-dimensional and unemotional at first sight. But despite the flat look this artistic style presents to Western eyes, it is designed to draw the viewer into a sense of the spiritual reality being represented. Icon art invites prayerful contemplation, moving the viewer to a communion with Christ, Our Lady, or the saint or angel portrayed.

Iconoclasm

In the eighth century a movement arose in the Eastern Church to banish the veneration of icons. Approved by Emperor Leo III in 726, this development led to iconoclasm, or image smashing. Its advocates argued that venerating images was forbidden by God in the First Commandment. They claimed it presented an obstacle to converting Jews and Muslims who considered honoring icons to be idolatry.

However, the Eastern monks opposed iconoclasm, as did the Western Church. It was always understood that the veneration of images of God and the saints was not fixed on the picture, but on the one represented by the picture. Iconoclasm was condemned by the Second Council of Nicaea (787). The empress Theodora restored the veneration of icons in 842.

Idolatry

The worshiping of statues of animals, humans, and cosmic bodies, representing false gods, is idolatry. Scripture notes many instances of the worship of idols with eyes that do not see, mouths that cannot talk, and ears that cannot hear (see Ps 115:4-8). The ancient Israelites were monotheists, believers in the one God.

Their most solemn prayer, the *shema* (see Dt 6:4), affirmed their faith in the one God who must be loved with all of one's mind, heart, and strength. But they were tempted to idolatry because of their contact with other cultures in which belief in many gods (polytheism) was the custom. God sent them the prophets, whose witness and preaching maintained the purity of the people's faith in one God.

The early gentile Christians, who

had been idolaters, needed special pastoral help to put idolatry behind them and worship one God: Father, Son, and Spirit. Idolatry today is most often manifested as treating money, sex, and power as absolutes to which one's whole life must be consecrated. But worshiping the real God is the only option that truly fulfills humanity.

Image of God

Genesis 1:27 teaches that God created man and woman in his own image. To be an image of God means that one can know the truth, will the good, master one's passions, and be inclined to God. Because humans are images of God, they have within them the dynamic push to truth and love, emotional energies that support this goal, and a sense of being drawn to God.

People also have another inner drive, due to original sin, that pulls them away from truth and love, allows the passions to run wild, and inclines them to evil. The interior drama between these two drives can be a story of victory for the image of God within people when they live by faith, walk in love, and allow divine grace to rule their lives.

Imitation of Christ

All growth in spirituality involves the imitation of Christ. Jesus has revealed what it really means to be human (see *Gaudium et Spes*, 22). Imitating

Christ's compassionate attitude for sinners, his methods for sharing the good news of the kingdom, and his humility enables people to learn the ways of holiness.

Since the acts of Christ are mysteries in the sense that they have a divine resonance, they are more than models for imitation. They are sources of sanctification. Hence to imitate Christ's deeds produces more than scripturally correct behavior in people's lives. People are gradually made new women and men through the graced experience of imitating the acts of Jesus, which are mysteries that contain transforming energies.

A spiritual classic by Thomas à Kempis (1380–1471) bears the title *The Imitation of Christ*. Composed in the late Middle Ages, this book has been one of the most popular and powerful means of helping people imitate Jesus and be changed by him.

Immaculate Conception

By God's will and the anticipated merits of Jesus Christ, the Virgin Mary was preserved from original sin from the first instant of her conception. Pope Pius IX defined the doctrine of the Immaculate Conception on December 8, 1854. But Church Fathers had preached the sinlessness of Mary, appealing to Scripture (see Gn 3:15; Lk 1:28), and the Eastern Church had always praised Mary as All-Holy (*panhagia*). Masses for the feast have been celebrated for centuries.

Because of a vision of Mary in 1834, St. Catherine Laboure popularized devotion to this truth through the wearing of what came to be called the Miraculous Medal. The medal bore the words, "O Mary, conceived without sin, pray for us." The truth was further supported when St. Bernadette asked the Lady her name during the Lourdes visions in 1858. Mary replied, "I am the Immaculate Conception."

Some people outside the Church misunderstand the doctrine as referring to the virginal conception and birth of Christ instead of Mary's being conceived without original sin.

Immersion, Baptism by

In this form of baptism, the body of the candidate is fully immersed in water three times along with the invocation, "I baptize you in the name of the Father, and of the Son, and of the Holy Spirit." The rites for baptism list immersion as the first way to baptize and infusion (pouring water on the head) as the second way.

Immortality of the Soul

To say that the soul is immortal means it cannot die. Virtually all cultures and religions throughout history have some form of belief in the immortality of the soul. The Old Testament has many references to the survival of the soul after death (see Eccl 12:7; Wis 3:1). The concept of *sheol* as the abode of the dead was an outgrowth of this belief.

The mission of Christ was essentially connected to belief in the soul's immortality and eternal life (see Mt 10:28; Mk 8:36-38; Lk 20:38). The Church's funeral liturgy further confirms this belief with the words that "life is changed, not taken away."

Impediment

When preparing people for the sacrament of marriage, care is taken to see that there are no impediments (or obstacles) that would render the marriage invalid.

Imposition of Hands

The placing of hands on the head of another person signifies the transmission of a blessing or a sacrament. The imposition of hands by the bishop at the ordination of a priest, along with the prayer of consecration, constitutes the essential acts of the sacrament of holy orders. Hands are also imposed at baptism, confirmation, and the anointing of the sick. In confession the priest raises his hand over the penitent for the words of absolution (forgiveness).

At Mass, the priest imposes hands over the bread and wine while praying that the Spirit will transform them into

Christ's Body and Blood. The use of hands for blessings and consecrations is found throughout the Scripture.

Imprimatur

From the Latin meaning "let it be printed," an imprimatur is given by a bishop for books on certain scriptural or religious topics. It is required for all Catholic versions of sacred Scripture and liturgical texts as well as religious books that will be used as textbooks or for public prayer. Otherwise, an imprimatur is not needed for every religious book.

Incardination

Every priest needs to be formally connected to a diocese or religious community; this connection is made through incardination. It occurs when a man is ordained a deacon for a diocese or a religious congregation. If a priest wants to change dioceses, the process called excardination allows for his release and an incardination into a new diocese. The practice of incardination is meant to stabilize the clergy and prevent freelancing or wandering priests.

Incarnation

When the Son of God took flesh in the womb of the Virgin Mary, the Incarnation happened (see Jn 1:14). Jesus taught that the Incarnation occurred because of God's love for the world; he does not come to condemn

the world, but to save it (see Jn 3:16-17). The Council of Chalcedon (A.D. 451) explained the Incarnation as the union of a human and a divine nature in the one divine Person of the Son of God. See also **Chalcedon, Council of; Trinity; Hypostatic Union**.

Incense

A fragrant resin found in warm climates, incense is put on burning charcoal, in a vessel called a censer, to create a sweet-smelling smoke. The rising of incense smoke symbolizes the outpouring of prayer of the worshipers. Incense is used at festal Masses, Benediction of the Blessed Sacrament and religious processions, solemn evening prayer, and the blessing of the body at funerals. It was used in temple worship in the Old Testament as well as in ancient pagan rituals.

Incest

Sexual relations between relatives or in-laws who are so closely related that they are not permitted to marry is incest (see 1 Cor 5:1, 4-5). The practice corrupts family life and is forbidden.

Index of Forbidden Books

A list of books considered hostile to the Church and dangerous for the faith of believers, the Index (or List) of Forbidden Books was first published by Pope Pius V in 1557. It was abolished in 1966.

Indulgences

The partial or full (plenary) remission of the temporal punishment due to sin, indulgences are granted for certain acts of piety designated by the Church. The guilt of sin is forgiven in the sacrament of penance, but damage of sin remains. The damage is an unhealthy attachment to creatures and requires the purification of the soul, which eliminates the temporal punishment due to sin. This purification can be achieved on earth by works of mercy, love, and penance—and by indulgences.

Indwelling of the Holy Spirit

At the Last Supper Jesus promised to send the Holy Spirit upon his people (see Jn 16:7). Numerous texts in the New Testament describe the Spirit as leading Christ, influencing the apostles, and guiding the members of the Church. This is not a mere external influence, but an interior one. The Spirit enters the soul—the most intimate part of a person—dwells there, and gives impulses that lead the person to a life of virtues and commitment to the kingdom. The Spirit calls for a free response of faith.

Inerrancy of Scripture

The books of Scripture teach the truths, without error, that God wanted to confide to the Bible for the sake of our salvation. This inerrancy is caused by the Holy Spirit's inspiration of the sacred writers. The Spirit used the talents of each author, but also accepted his limitations. The human author's lack of knowledge in some areas did not interfere with the inerrant truths of salvation the Spirit wanted to convey (see *Catechism*, par. 106-7). See also **Inspiration of Scripture.**

Infallibility

Christ sent the Holy Spirit to the Church so that the purity of faith and truth, handed on by the apostles, would be maintained. Jesus gave the Church a teaching office—a Magisterium of pope and bishops—to help God's people profess the faith without error. The gift of infallibility is the expression of this divine concern.

The pope speaks infallibly when he proclaims by a definitive act a doctrine pertaining to faith and morals. This infallibility is also present when the bishops, together with the pope, exercise their teaching office in an ecumenical council (see *Catechism*, par. 888-92).

Infant Baptism

The practice of infant baptism has a long history in the Church. There is explicit testimony about it in the second century. It is possible that babies were baptized in New Testament times when whole households received baptism (see Acts 16:15; 1 Cor 1:16). Baptizing infants illustrates the sheer gratuitousness of salvation and gives the baby the priceless gift of becoming a child of God.

Infinite

Meaning without limits, the term *infinite* applies to the unlimited being of God. Having the fullness of unity, goodness, truth, and beauty, God embraces to an infinite degree these qualities he wishes to share with us.

Initiation, Christian

The Rite of Christian Initiation of Adults (RCIA) comprises the various rituals, ceremonies, community building, and catechetical teachings that prepare candidates for baptism, confirmation, and the Eucharist. This preparation usually lasts about a year and includes sponsors and the support of the parish community. The preparation leads up to the Easter Vigil, where the sacraments are received.

Inquisition

The name given to Church courts that tried people for heresy, the Inquisition was established by Pope Gregory IX in 1233 to combat the Albigensian heresy. The inquisitors tried to determine whether or not the person was a heretic. Punishments such as fines, imprisonment, confiscation of property,

and torture to cure the heretic were handled by the civil authorities.

Church and state justified this procedure in the name of preserving doctrinal truths and social stability. The Church established an inquisition office in Rome in 1542, but this office was separated from civil punishments. Today that department is the Congregation for the Doctrine of the Faith. Pope John Paul II has formally apologized for the excesses of the Inquisition.

I.N.R.I.

Above the head of Christ on most crucifixes is the inscription "I.N.R.I." These are the initials for the Latin words *Iesus Nazarenus Rex Iudaeorum*, translated "Jesus of Nazareth, King of the Jews." The words come from the order of Pilate that this sign should be placed on the cross in Hebrew, Latin, and Greek (see Jn 19:19).

Inspiration of Scripture

Derived from the Latin for "breathing into," the term *inspiration* implies a spiritual or emotional influence exercised on someone. The words of Scripture have been written under the inspiration of the Holy Spirit. The human authors of Scripture, with both their strengths and limitations, were inspired by the Spirit. Scripture is the Word of God in the words of human authors. See also **Inerrancy of Scripture**.

Institutes, Religious

Men and women who live the consecrated life belong to a religious institute, which may be a religious order or congregation. The members have a liturgical character; live in common; profess the evangelical counsels of poverty, chastity, and obedience; and witness to Christ's union with the Church.

Institutes, Secular

Members of secular institutes follow the consecrated life, not in a monastery or convent, but in a secular setting. They are dedicated to evangelization and they wish to be a leaven in the world, informing it with the spirit of the gospel.

Intercommunion

When churches of different denominations invite members to Holy Communion, they are practicing intercommunion. The Catholic Church welcomes to Holy Communion only those who are in full communion with the Church and forbids Catholics to take Holy Communion in other churches. There are exceptions for non-Catholic Christians who have a serious spiritual need, have no church of their own available, and believe in the real presence.

The Catholic Church does invite members of Orthodox Churches to Communion since their doctrine and practice of priesthood and Eucharist is valid, but notes that members of their Churches should follow the rules of their congregations on this matter. Intercommunion issues arise at weddings, funerals, and ordinations at which members of other faiths are present. Usually, the printed program has an advisory note about this in the section before Communion.

Internal Forum

Absolute confidentiality is required in the internal forum—the *place* of confiding and judging—in the sacrament of confession. The seal of confession may not be broken.

In Vitro Fertilization

Sterile couples without children suffer greatly and seek new techniques to have babies. One technique that brings about the fertilization of a woman's egg by the man's sperm, *in vitro* ("in a dish") fertilization, is an artificial means of conception.

The process entrusts the life and identity of the embryo to doctors and biologists. Technology replaces what the conjugal act was meant to do and takes over the origin and destiny of a human person. For these reasons, *in vitro* fertilization is morally unacceptable.

Nevertheless, other scientific solutions to sterility should be encouraged so long as they serve human dignity and are in accord with God's plan for marriage and conception.

Irenicism

From the Greek word for "peace," irenicism describes the reconciling attitude one needs for ecumenical dialogue. See also **Ecumenism**.

Islam

Founded by Muhammed in 622, Islam is the religion of the Muslims. The word means "submission to God's will." Islam is a monotheistic religion.

Muslims follow the Koran, a book that incorporates what is believed to be the final revelation of *Allah* (God) to the world. The Koran honors many of the Old Testament prophets and considers Jesus to be a prophet. It also has a high regard for Mary the mother of Jesus.

The "five pillars" of the Muslim religion are (1) belief in Allah and Muhammed, his prophet; (2) prayer at dawn, noon, afternoon, sunset, and nighttime; (3) charity for the poor; (4) fasting; (5) a one-time pilgrimage to Mecca. Islam today is one of the world's largest religions, numbering about one billion followers. The Vatican's secretariat for non-Christian religions maintains a dialogue with Muslim religious leaders.

Israel

Scripture teaches that God chose the Israelite people to be the first bearers of his plan for the salvation of the world. Their name comes from their patriarch Jacob, whose alternate name was Israel. Today, Israel is the name for the Jewish state that came into existence on May 15, 1948, as the result of the partition of Palestine by the United Nations.

J

Jacob

The twin brother of Esau, the patriarch Jacob, whose other name is Israel, sired twelve sons who became the heads of the twelve tribes of Israel. See also **Israel**.

Jansenism

Named after its major theoretician, Bishop Cornelius Jansen, the movement known as Jansenism originated in Belgium and France in the seventeenth century. Its negative, rigoristic theology and spirituality was based upon a misreading of the thought of St. Augustine, especially his teachings on grace. The adherents held that Jesus did not die for everyone; human freedom is gone; temptations are overwhelming; and only the purest can receive Communion.

This approach fostered scrupulosity, burdened conscience, and encouraged unreasonable penances. Several popes condemned the movement, beginning with Pope Innocent X in 1654, but its puritanical influence lasted for many years.

Jehovah

The Hebrew prophets commonly used the name Yahweh for God. In English this is sometimes expressed as Jehovah. Both words are from the Hebrew YHWH, the name given by God to Moses at the burning bush. Such was the reverence postexilic Jews had for God's name that they did not pronounce Yahweh or Jehovah, but a substitute title *Adonai,* which means "my Lord."

Jerusalem

The name of the holy city of Jerusalem means "city of peace." It is a sacred city for Jews, Christians, and Muslims. In biblical times it became the chief city in Palestine because of its fortresslike geography along a trade route between Egypt and the eastern kingdoms, as well as its reliable water supply.

Under David and Solomon, Jerusalem became the capital for the United Kingdom of Israel and Judah. The Jewish temple, where the prophets preached, was built there. Jesus completed his ministry and paschal mystery in this city. The Romans destroyed Jerusalem in A.D. 70. It subsequently underwent several destructions and rebuildings over the centuries.

Jerusalem, Council of

Acts chapter fifteen describes the Council of Jerusalem, convened to settle the dispute as to whether Gentile converts needed circumcision and a commitment to Jewish dietary laws as a condition for their entry into Christianity. The council decided that they did not, and thus opened the way for evangelizing Gentiles without imposing these unnecessary rules for Christians. The covenant sign for Christians was to be baptism, not circumcision.

Jesuits

Founded by St. Ignatius of Loyola as the Society of Jesus in 1534, the Jesuits have been one of the Church's most influential religious orders. Their stress on spirituality through the Spiritual Exercises of St. Ignatius continues to be one of the most fruitful methods ever devised to answer the call to holiness. Their missionary endeavors in the New World as well as in China and India remain legendary. Their distinguished commitment to Catholic education in high schools, colleges, and universities has placed them historically among the greatest contributors to human and Christian culture. Their list of saints includes Francis Xavier, Aloysius Gonzaga, Peter Canisius, Isaac Jogues, and the North American Martyrs.

Jesus Christ

The Son of God who became man in the womb of the Virgin Mary by the power of the Holy Spirit, Jesus Christ lived, died, rose from the dead, ascended into heaven, and sent the Holy Spirit— all for the salvation of the world. He will come again in glory to judge the living and the dead. Jesus means "God saves." Christ means "anointed one" or "Messiah." See also **Incarnation**.

Jesus Seminar

A radical group of Scripture scholars, the Jesus Seminar has applied extreme forms of historical criticism to determine which Gospel words and deeds Jesus actually said and did. Most of them have judged that the Virgin Birth and the Resurrection did not happen and that the majority of Christ's reported words and deeds never occurred. Mainstream Scripture scholars have mounted forceful critiques discrediting the Jesus Seminar's assumptions and conclusions. (For further study, see Luke Timothy Johnson, *The Real Jesus: The Misguided Quest for the Historical Jesus and the Truth of the Traditional Gospels*, Harper, 1996).

Jewish People

See **Judaism**.

John's Gospel, St.

The fourth Gospel was most likely written about the year A.D. 90 and is different in style from the first three Gospels. The first twelve chapters are built around seven signs or miracles of Jesus by which he manifested his "glory," that is, divinity. Christ's teaching method in this Gospel often takes place in dialogues, such as his conversations with St. Nicodemus (see Jn 3:1-21) and the woman at the well (see Jn 4:1-42), and his dialogue with the crowds about the bread of life (see Jn 6:22-71).

The last nine chapters illumine the sign of the cross through the unique way that St. John chose to report the paschal mystery. The whole Gospel is radiant with the power and presence of the risen Christ.

John the Baptist, St.

Born of St. Elizabeth and St. Zachary, St. John the Baptist was sanctified in the womb when Mary, pregnant with Jesus, visited Elizabeth (see Lk 1:44). St. John was a prophet in the style and force of Elijah and was the immediate forerunner of his cousin Jesus. He lived the ascetic life in the desert, preached repentance, and called people to symbolize their moral conversion by receiving baptism in the Jordan River.

When Jesus came to him for baptism, St. John protested, but Jesus persisted, saying that it was fitting as part of God's plan. The Baptist was arrested and ultimately beheaded for condemning King Herod for adultery.

Jordan River

The part of the Jordan River that figures in Scripture is the section from the south end of the Sea of Galilee to the north end of the Dead Sea. Called the "liquid backbone of Palestine," the Jordan was famously the setting where Joshua led God's people into the Promised Land (see Jos 3:14-17) and also of the Baptism of Jesus (see Mt 3:13-17).

Joseph, St.

Adoptive father of Jesus, St. Joseph is the husband of the Virgin Mary. St. Matthew's Gospel looks at the birth of Jesus from St. Joseph's perspective. It is in St. Matthew that an angel appears to St. Joseph three times: to assure him that the conception of Jesus is of divine origin, to urge him to take mother and Child to Egypt, and to instruct him to bring them back to Nazareth (see Mt 1:20-21; 2:13, 19-20).

St. Joseph was a carpenter who witnessed the birth and circumcision of Jesus, as well as the loss and finding of Christ in the Temple. The apocryphal book *The Protoevangelium of James* pictures St. Joseph as an old widower with children when he marries Mary. This tradition is used by the Eastern Church to explain why the Gospels could speak of the "brothers and sisters" of Jesus, while maintaining belief in the perpetual virginity of Mary.

Jubilee
See **Holy Year.**

Judaism
Encompassing the religious, ethnic, and political identity of the Jewish people, Judaism has roots that go back to Abraham, their father in faith, and the patriarch Jacob/Israel who fathered the leaders of the twelve tribes. Moses' covenant with God at Sinai specified their status as God's people. Joshua, Saul, David, and Solomon established their political identity. After the Babylonian Captivity, Ezra renewed their biblical covenant and began the building of the second temple (538 B.C.), and Nehemiah administered the rebuilding of Jerusalem (445-433 B.C.).

The developed Jewish religion of this latter period is sometimes called "second temple Judaism." Since the destruction of the temple in A.D. 70 and the subsequent diaspora (the scattering of the Jews to many nations), Judaism has spread all over the world. See also **Israel.**

Judas
The apostle who betrayed Jesus, Judas never understood the real meaning of Christ's messiahship, which he thought of in political rather than spiritual terms. He died a violent death, described by Scripture in two differing accounts (see Mt 27:5; Acts 1:18).

Judgment
Scripture teaches that ultimately all people will be judged by God according to the way they lived. The *Catechism* speaks of a particular judgment that occurs at each individual's death (par. 1021-22). At this point the person goes either to heaven, purgatory, or hell, depending on the condition of the soul, as illustrated by the parable of the rich man and Lazarus (see Lk 16:22-23) and the destiny of the good thief (see Lk 23:43).

At the Last (or General) Judgment, the dead will rise from the grave and Christ's second coming will occur. The meaning of salvation history will be revealed, God's victory over evil will be made clear, and the new heavens and new earth will be established (see *Catechism,* par. 1021-50).

Just War Theory
Historically the Church has tried to mitigate the horrors of war, such as genocide, ethnic cleansing, bombing of civilians, and inhumane treatment of wounded soldiers and prisoners of war. The *Catechism* (par. 2309) presents an outline of the strict conditions for legiti-

mate defense by military force. It notes
that the power of modern means of
destruction weigh heavily in any evaluation of the conditions for a just war.

Justice

One of the four cardinal virtues, justice
is rendering to God and people what is
due to them. While ideas of justice are
connected to what lawmakers, judges,
and lawyers determine and also what
social concerns for the poor require,
there are also Christian concepts of justice in everyday relationships. In this
latter area justice needs to be seen along
with the moderating virtues of love and
mercy. See also **Social Justice**.

Justification

The process by which a sinner is made
right before God, justification comes
about by the power of the Holy Spirit.
The Spirit prompts conversion, detachment from sin, and cooperation
between God's grace and human freedom, and applies the merits of Christ's
passion and resurrection to the justified
in baptism. The human response to this
work of the Spirit is grace-supported
faith and graced good works that
respond to God's call to virtue.

Kenosis

A Greek word meaning "emptying," *kenosis* refers to the Son of God's self-emptying of his status of glory in becoming a man. It involves the obedient humility that led Jesus to the cross and became the source of his glorification and the manifestation of his divinity so that all people in heaven and earth and under the earth are prompted to acclaim him as Lord. *Kenosis* is an attitude to which all followers of Christ are invited (see Phil 2:5-11).

Kerygma

A Greek word meaning a "proclaimed message," *kerygma* has acquired, for Christians, a specific application to the proclamation of the Good News or gospel of Jesus Christ. Homilists at Mass and teachers of religion in classrooms or other settings are urged to have the spirit and content of the *kerygma* in their presentations so that the faith of listeners may be stirred up.

Kingdom of God (or of Heaven)

The primary focus of Christ's preaching and teaching was the kingdom of God (or of heaven). It is a reality that embraces God's rule over creation and history, salvation from sin, the gift of divine life, and the call to live the virtues of love, justice, and mercy in all relationships (see Mt 6:33; Rom 14:17). The Church is the seed and beginning of God's kingdom on earth, and the Eucharist contains the reality of the kingdom. In the Our Father, believers pray, "Thy kingdom come."

Knights of Columbus

The largest Catholic layman's organization in the world, the Knights of Columbus fosters a life of faith and social conscience among its members and makes numerous outstanding contributions to the apostolates of the Church. It was founded by Father Michael J. McGivney in 1882.

Knights of Malta

Historically the Knights of Malta began as a military order in Jerusalem in A.D. 1100 for the purpose of caring for the sick and pilgrims in the Holy Land. Their original name was the Knights of St. John of Jerusalem, but it was changed to Knights of Malta during their sovereign occupation of the island (1530–1798). Today the organization ministers to the spiritual development of its members, both men and women, and devotes itself to works of justice and charity.

Knights of the Holy Sepulchre

Founded during the First Crusade in 1099, the Knights of the Holy Sepulchre committed themselves to protect and defend the city of Jerusalem and the church of the Holy Sepulchre. Today the organization looks after the spiritual development of its members and the needs—financial or otherwise—of the Christian shrines in the Holy Land.

Know-Nothingism

From 1840 to 1856, a secret society of American Protestants tried to stop the wave of Catholic immigrants to the United States—and to restrict the civil rights of the ones already here. They were called "Know Nothings" because they answered, "I know nothing," to questions about their secretive affairs. After losing a national election in 1856, the movement died out.

Koinonia

A Greek word meaning community, *koinonia* applies to the dynamic movement of the first Christian converts to form communities of prayer, celebrate the Eucharist, and engage in the voluntary sharing of goods and fellowship with one another. Ever since, the Church has emphasized the role of forming and building community in Christ in parishes, dioceses, and the universal Church.

Koran

See **Islam**.

Kyrie Eleison

Meaning in Greek "Lord, have mercy," the words *Kyrie Eleison* were for many centuries retained in Greek during Latin Masses, but now the phrase is in the vernacular in the contemporary liturgies.

L

Laity

Also called "lay faithful" in Church documents, laity refers to all baptized members of the Church who belong to the common priesthood of believers but not the ordained ministerial priesthood. St. Peter addresses the laity of his time as God's holy people called to praise God (see 1 Pt 2:9-10). Vatican II's constitution on the Church, *Lumen Gentium,* devotes its second chapter to the "People of God," in which there is a special emphasis on the lay faithful.

The laity, in their own way, share in the priestly, prophetic, and kingly mission of Christ and the Church in the world. The lay faithful are called to holiness as well as to evangelize and sanctify the world, especially within the areas where they can be active. They have the support of the Holy Spirit, the Church, the sacraments, and the community in this mission.

Lamb of God

Biblical times honored shepherd culture as both an economic and a religious reality. Scripture uses images of shepherds and sheep to illustrate divine truths. God is often called the Shepherd of Israel. Lambs figured centrally in the Passover meal.

St. John the Baptist called Jesus the "Lamb of God" (see Jn 1:35-36). St. Paul confirmed this title when he named Jesus the "Passover sacrificial Lamb" (see 1 Cor 5:7). An actual lamb could not redeem anyone, but Jesus replaced the animal of the Passover sacrifice and became the true Lamb able to save the world.

Isaiah 53:7 supplies Old Testament prophetic language to illustrate the Messiah as the saving Lamb. In the Mass, the priest holds up the consecrated host at Communion and says, "Behold the Lamb of God." Jesus is not only a saving "Lamb," but the saving food of the Eucharist for our spiritual nourishment.

La Salette, Our Lady of

The Virgin Mary appeared to two children in La Salette, France, in 1846. The apparition was approved by the Church in 1851 and the Virgin's message has been supported and advanced by the Missionaries of La Salette ever since.

Last Judgment

See **Judgment**.

Last Sacraments

Also known as last rites, the last sacraments may include confession, confirmation (if needed), anointing of the sick, and Holy Communion. The anointing of the sick, however, once known as extreme unction, may be given whenever serious illness or surgery occurs, not just at the apparent end of one's life. The final Eucharist is called Viaticum (meaning "for the journey"), a Communion for the voyage into the next life.

Last Supper

See **Lord's Supper.**

Lateran Basilica, St. John

The pope's cathedral for the diocese of Rome, St. John Lateran Basilica is the pope's official church. His authority, as successor of St. Peter, comes from being the bishop of Rome, from which he also serves as universal pastor of the whole Church.

Latin Mass

Since the fourth century the Latin Mass, with attendant rituals often revised, has been the prevailing liturgical language and practice for the Western Church. With Vatican II's decision to introduce the vernacular into the liturgy, the dominance of the Latin Mass has receded. Occasionally, some parishes will have a Latin Mass according to the New Rituals (*Novus Ordo*). Pope John Paul II has approved the use of the old Latin Mass codified by Pope St. Pius V in the sixteenth century. Its

use must be approved by a local bishop for pastoral reasons.

Lauds

A word that means "praise," Lauds is another name for Morning Prayer in the Liturgy of the Hours.

Law, Moral

Applied both to natural law and the laws of God contained in the Ten Commandments and the moral teachings of Christ and the New Testament, the moral law is an objective guide for one's moral and spiritual life. The natural law, which God plants in every human soul and is a reflection of the divine law, finds scriptural expression in the Ten Commandments. Every human being can know the natural law by using reason. Christ's two commandments— love of God and of neighbor—are the Christian basis of all moral laws. The Sermon on the Mount is a major expression of the moral law.

Lectern

The reading stand for proclamation of the scriptural texts at liturgy, the lectern holds a prominent place in the sanctuary. It is also the place where the homily is customarily delivered.

Lectionary

The book of readings from Scripture to be used at liturgies, the lectionary contains the cycles of readings used over a three-year period.

Legion of Mary

An association of laity convened under the patronage of the Blessed Mother, the Legion of Mary was founded by Frank Duff in Dublin in 1921. The organization emphasizes a strong spiritual life, inspired by the Virgin Mary, as a preparation for a wide variety of apostolic endeavors on behalf of the Church's mission in the world.

Lent

A major liturgical season of penance and prayer, Lent lasts for forty days, beginning with Ash Wednesday and continuing until Easter. Ash Wednesday and Good Friday are days of fast and abstinence from meat. All Fridays of Lent are abstinence days.

Catholics are encouraged in Lent to increase their spiritual activities, such as attending daily Mass; going to confession; and engaging in spiritual exercises such as making the Stations of the Cross, listening to Lenten sermons, or making retreats. Also desired are increased acts of charity and charitable giving. Lent should be seen as a spiritual journey of faith that leads and prepares one to celebrate the paschal mystery on Holy Thursday, Good Friday, and the Easter Vigil. Since Lent is also the final phase of preparing candidates for the sacraments of initiation at the Easter Vigil, all Catholics are invited to walk with them in prayer and communal support at this important time in their lives.

Liberation Theology

Found mainly in Latin America, liberation theology is a form of religious reflection meant to enable the poor to seek freedom from poverty and political-economic structures that prevent them from living with human dignity and fulfillment in their cultures. The theology often uses the story of the Exodus liberation of Israel from Egypt as a scriptural model. Some forms of the theology employ strategies and ideas from Marxism that seem to Church authorities inappropriate for Catholic theology and pastoral practice. Generally, liberation theology and the Church's social teachings have been coming closer together for the common goal of social justice and a preferential option for the poor.

Liberty, Religious

Freedom of religion is a commonplace in modern democracies, but such religious liberty is often prohibited in totalitarian societies. At Vatican II the bishops approved the "Declaration on

Religious Freedom," which teaches that governments should not restrain religions so long as their beliefs and practices do no harm to the common good. Religious liberty is based on the premise that each person is called to look for the truth, and one part of that search is the truth of faith. The state should do nothing to prevent this quest and in fact should realize that the authentic growth of religion benefits both the state and society.

Life, Spiritual
See **Spirituality**.

Limbo
Often thought to be the place where unbaptized babies go when they die, limbo was a speculative teaching meant to console parents who faced this unhappy situation. The *Catechism* takes up the issue of children and the unborn who have died without baptism by noting that God works through the sacraments, but is not bound by the sacraments. The Church entrusts children who have died without baptism to the mercy of God, who desires salvation for all (see 1 Tm 2:3-4). Recalling that Christ wanted the children to come to him (see Mk 10:14), the faithful hope there is a saving path for the children who have died without baptism (see *Catechism*, par. 1257, 1261).

Litany
A soothing, repetitive prayer in which a short prayer response is made to a series of differing invocations, the litany has proven to be an aid to meditation on the mysteries of Christ, the Blessed Mother, and the other saints. All ordination ceremonies call for the Litany of the Saints just before the imposition of hands. There are many devotional litanies suitable for prayer on different occasions.

Literal Sense of Scripture
Vatican II's constitution on interpreting the Scriptures (*Dei Verbum*) teaches that the first step in determining the meaning of the text is to seek out its literal meaning. This requires looking for the intention of the inspired author. It also means identifying the nature of the text as to whether it is history, parable, poetry, song, wisdom saying, or short story. The literal meaning can be communicated through various literary forms, which take unique shapes in particular cultures. See also **Inerrancy of Scripture; Inspiration of Scripture**.

Liturgy
Based on the Greek words *laos* (people) and *ergon* (work), the term *liturgy* refers to a work of God's people in praising and worshiping the Lord. Liturgy's greatest acts are the celebrations of the sacraments and above all

the Eucharist, the summit and source of Christian life. The celebrations of the Christian mysteries of salvation continue God's saving work begun in the Old Testament and perfected and realized by Christ in the New Testament.

Through the Church and the sacraments, the liturgy assembles the priests and the lay faithful in a community of faith and prayer where the Trinity is adored and the graces of salvation are received. The section of the *Catechism* called "The Celebration of the Christian Mystery" explores the Church's teaching about liturgy. Part I discusses the foundations of liturgy. Part II applies these teachings to liturgy as it is celebrated in the seven sacraments.

Liturgy, Divine

The name for the celebration of the Eucharist in the Eastern Church, the divine liturgy is a transcendent expression of the mystery of God's presence and action during worship.

Liturgy of the Hours

A way to extend the meaning and impact of the celebration of the Eucharist throughout the day and night, the Liturgy of the Hours illustrates the body of Christ at prayer. Traditionally it has been called the Divine Office. Designed for community prayer, it may also be done alone. The center of these hours is the psalms and readings from Scripture, Church fathers, and saints. Its main sections are the office of readings, morning prayer, daytime prayer, evening prayer, and night prayer.

Religious orders and congregations commit themselves to chanting this liturgy in choir, at least for morning and evening prayer. Contemplative orders chant the full liturgy. Parish priests generally pray the office in private. A one-volume book of Christian prayer, often used by the lay faithful, contains morning and evening prayer. As the prayer of the Church, the liturgy of the hours is a powerful source of growth in faith and sanctification.

Lives of the Saints

From the earliest days of Christianity, brief biographies of martyrs and other saints were written to inspire the readers to more courageous and faith-filled living. Saints' lives are vivid interpretations of the Gospels. They show how Christ's example and teachings can really be lived by rich and poor, men and women, priests and laity, nuns and monks, hermits and religious communities, soldiers and simple folk, kings and laborers, married and single. Sanctity is within the reach of everyone. (For further study, see the four-volume work by Fr. Alban Butler, *The Lives of the Saints*.)

Logos

A Greek word meaning "word," *logos* was used by St. John in the opening chapter of his Gospel. He wrote that the Son of God was the Word who existed as God before the Incarnation. This Word became flesh in Jesus Christ and lived among us to save us (see Jn 1:1-14).

Lord's Prayer

Jesus often went aside to pray. The apostles were impressed by the witness of his prayer. One of the disciples asked Jesus to teach them to pray (see Lk 11:1). Jesus responded by teaching them the Our Father, also known as the Lord's Prayer.

St. Luke presents a version with five petitions (see Lk 11:2-4). St. Matthew gives a more developed prayer with seven petitions (see Mt 6:9-13). It is St. Matthew's text that the Church uses.

The *Catechism* (par. 2803-56) gives a reflection on the seven petitions. Many saints, such as St. Augustine and St. Teresa of Avila, have written extensive meditations on the Lord's Prayer. It has been considered a perfect prayer since it contains the essential attitude and content of all prayer.

Lord's Supper

On Holy Thursday night, Jesus gathered his apostles in an upper room in Jerusalem for their last supper together, now known as the Lord's Supper, before his passion and death. At that meal, Jesus instituted the Eucharist. While the setting was a meal and the central mystery was the changing of bread and wine into Christ's Body and Blood, the event also had a sacrificial character because Jesus noted that his Body would be given up for them and the cup of wine was his Blood to be shed for them (see Lk 22:19-20). See also **Eucharist**.

Lourdes Apparitions

In 1858, the Virgin Mary appeared eighteen times to St. Bernadette Soubirous in the grotto at Lourdes, aside the River Gave in southern France. When asked her identity, Mary said, "I am the Immaculate Conception." Mary instructed St. Bernadette to "drink from the spring." The young woman struggled with the earth but found only muddy water at first. By evening a spring was flowing and still does to this day—a source of miraculous, physical healing for some.

St. Bernadette entered a contemplative convent and died a saint. Lourdes has become one of the Church's greatest pilgrimage shrines, attracting many millions every year, some looking for physical healing, most coming for a renewal of their religious faith.

Love

In any number of ways, Scripture extols love of God and neighbor as the greatest of the virtues. St. Paul reached the heights of poetic eloquence in his praise of love (see 1 Cor 13:1-13). St. John said many things about God, but finally summed it all up in a simple sentence: "God is love" (1 Jn 4:8). Jesus taught that love of God and neighbor are the two greatest commandments (see Mt 22:37-40).

Saints have echoed this teaching of the Scripture ever since. Mother Teresa of Calcutta put it plainly: "God does not expect great deeds from us, only everyday acts done with great love."

Lucifer

His name meaning "light bearer," Lucifer (or Satan) was the most brilliant of angels, but he was filled with pride, rebelled against God, and was driven from heaven. Isaiah 14:12 seems to refer to Lucifer's downfall, and Jesus echoes Isaiah's verse when he says he saw Satan fall like lightning from heaven (see Lk 10:18). Revelation 12:7-9 describes the rebellion and fall of the bad angels.

Luke's Gospel, St.

Probably written around the year 80, St. Luke's Gospel displays great literary artistry and human appeal. His infancy narrative, with its emphasis on Mary and the shepherds, has profoundly influenced the popular vision of Christmas. The text has variously been characterized as the Gospel of prayer, of women, of compassion, and of forgiveness.

Since St. Luke sets so many powerful scenes at meals, his Gospel seems to make the meal a principal locale for reconciliation. The book is part one of a two-book series that includes the Acts of the Apostles. His audience is primarily Gentiles.

Lumen Gentium

The Vatican II constitution on the Church, *Lumen Gentium,* lays the theological groundwork for appreciating the meaning and role of the Church as a sacrament of salvation. Its opening chapter establishes the Church as a divine mystery, called into being by the Father, established by Christ, and manifested and sustained by the Spirit. The next chapter deals with the Church as the People of God, called to be a holy community that will witness to the world about salvation.

Subsequent chapters deal with other aspects of the Church, such as hierarchy, religious life, the call to holiness, and an excellent section on the Virgin Mary. *Lumen Gentium* should be studied in conjunction with *Gaudium et Spes,* the constitution about the pastoral role of the Church in the modern world.

M

Madonna

Italian for "My Lady," Madonna has become an affectionate title for the Virgin Mary, especially in reference to her virginal motherhood of Jesus. Numerous paintings and sculptures by famous artists have portrayed Mary and Jesus as Madonna and Child.

Magi

Meaning "wise men," the term *Magi* refers to the three wise men who came from the East to worship the newborn Jesus. Their story is told in Matthew 2:1-12.

The Magi arrived in Jerusalem and met with King Herod to ask him about the newborn king of the Jews, for they had seen his star in the East. Herod consulted the priests and scribes, who told him that the Messiah would be born in Bethlehem. Hearing this news, the Magi went to Bethlehem, found the Child, did him homage, and gave him gifts of gold, frankincense, and myrrh. They did not return to Herod but, directed by an angel, left by a different route.

Magisterium

The official teaching office of the Church, the Magisterium is composed of the pope and bishops as successors of St. Peter and the apostles. Guided, enlightened, and protected by the ever-present Holy Spirit, the members of the Magisterium preserve the teachings of Apostolic Tradition and Scripture. They offer authoritative interpretations of the deposit of faith to serve the pastoral needs of God's people.

Magnificat

When Mary visited her cousin St. Elizabeth to help her with the coming birth of her child, the exchange between the two women concluded with Mary's hymn of praise (see Lk 1:46-55). Called the *Magnificat* because of Mary's opening words, "My soul magnifies," the canticle is a masterpiece of scriptural poetry and praise.

Mary contrasts her humble station with the mighty works of God, who raises up the lowly and casts down the proud. She thanks God for the gift of the Incarnation: "The Mighty One has done great things for me" (Lk 1:49 NAB). So treasured is this hymn by the Church that it is sung at evening prayer in the Liturgy of the Hours every day all over the world.

Manna

During Israel's forty years in the desert after the liberation from Egypt, the people complained about the need for bread. Moses brought their petition to God, who graced them with the miracle of the manna, a sticky substance that fell from the skies each day and could be ground and baked into bread (see Ex 16:13-22). Archaeologists speculate the manna might have been the secretion of insects who feed on the tamarisk tree and secrete the excess in the form of honeydew manna that gathers on the ground much as Scripture describes.

In St. John's Gospel, the people fed by the multiplication of the loaves cite the manna miracle to Jesus during a dialogue with him. Jesus contrasts the manna that disappears with the eternal bread he plans to give them (see Jn 6:31-35).

Mark's Gospel, St.

The shortest of the Gospels, St. Mark's account was probably written around A.D. 70, just before the destruction of Jerusalem. St. Mark's emphasis on the discipleship of the cross in Christ's teaching and his lengthy presentation of Christ's passion have led some to characterize his Gospel as a passion narrative with a preface. He speaks of Jesus as the Son of God in his opening line, and this is echoed by the centurion at the cross: "Truly this man was the Son of God" (see Mk 15:39).

Most scholars today teach that St. Mark's Gospel came first, but several give this position to St. Matthew's Gospel. Because of its brevity, St. Mark has occasionally been recited by heart by major actors in one-man shows. Some believe this approach recovers the sense of gospel proclamation, which was the first way the preached Gospels were experienced.

Marks of the Church

The four marks of the Church—one, holy, Catholic, apostolic—are inseparably linked to each other. They are always found in the Church and are essential to the Church's mission. Only faith can perceive this.

The holiness of the Church's saints, its stability, and its charitable endeavors testify to her credibility and divine mission. But the sinfulness of the members demonstrate that the marks are not wholly realized. Hence the four marks are both a reality and a challenge. (For further study read the *Catechism,* par. 813-65.)

Marriage Encounter

A movement to deepen the relationship between husbands and wives, Marriage Encounter weekends include conferences, testimonies, dialogues, counseling, prayer, and the celebration of the Eucharist. The movement has been the admirable occasion of graces that heal, strengthen, and animate many marriages.

Marriage, Sacrament of

Designated by the Church as a sacrament of communion, the sacrament of marriage signifies the union of Christ and his Church. From this sacrament flow the graces that spouses need to love each other as Jesus loves the Church. The sacrament perfects the love of the spouses, provides the divine help to maintain the lifelong stability of the marriage, and offers the spouses the help needed for the journey to eternal life. In the sacrament, the spouses proclaim their permanent conjugal love for each other and their commitment to cooperate with God in having children and raising them in faith, hope, love, and all that is needed for their human and spiritual fulfillment.

Martyr

The word *martyr* literally means "witness" and applies especially to men and women who have accepted execution rather than give up their faith. Blood martyrdom has been characteristic of Church witness since New Testament times and continues into the modern era. The martyr bears witness to Jesus Christ and his saving work, as well as to the truths of the Christian faith. People who are martyred for these reasons before the possibility of baptism by water are said to have received baptism by blood.

Mary, The Virgin

The Church upholds the perpetual virginity of Mary as a matter of faith. Mary is a virgin before, during, and after the birth of Jesus. Objections to this teaching come from those who conclude that the New Testament references to the brothers and sisters of Jesus illustrate that Mary had other children (see Mk 3:31-35; 1 Cor 9:5; Gal 1:19).

The Eastern Church argues that these were children by St. Joseph from his first marriage as noted in the ancient book called *Protoevangelium of James.* The Western Church follows the teaching of St. Jerome given in his book *Against Helvidius,* where he argues that they were cousins, not siblings, noting that the Greek word may be translated either way. The *Catechism* (par. 502-7) outlines five faith-informed values that flow from Mary's perpetual virginity.

Mary, Mother of God

The angel Gabriel appeared to Mary and invited her to accept the conception of God's Son in her womb by the power of the Holy Spirit. Mary agreed in faith to this call, and so she became the Mother of God. In the year 431 the Council of Ephesus confirmed this revealed truth of faith by declaring that Mary is the *Theotokos,* or God-bearer. See also **Annunciation.**

Mass

One of the names for the celebration of the Eucharist, the term Mass comes from the Latin expression, *"Ite, missa est"* ("Go, the Mass is ended"). It implies the missionary nature of Eucharist, in that the participants in the celebration should go forth and engage in apostolic works of love, justice, and mercy toward others.

Matthew's Gospel, St.

Written probably around A.D. 80, the Gospel attributed to St. Matthew has been very influential in the life of the Church. Some scholars maintain the book was written in Antioch of Syria, where it would address Jewish converts to Christianity at a time when many Gentile converts were being made and the pastoral issues dividing them needed answers.

The first two chapters deal with the birth of Jesus. The body of the text is divided into five sections marked by s ermons by Jesus, the most famous of which is the first discourse, or Sermon on the Mount (see Mt chapters 5–7). The other four sermons deal with missionary work, the parables of the kingdom, church order, and the end times. As in all the Gospels, St. Matthew's final section covers the passion and resurrection of Jesus.

Mediator

By reason of his reconciling work in his passion, death, and resurrection, Jesus Christ is the one Mediator between God and all people (see 1 Tm 2:5).

Mediatrix of Graces

The Virgin Mary is sometimes called the Mediatrix of Graces by virtue of her cooperation with the work of her Son. Her maternal mediation in no way obscures the unique mediation of Christ. Hers is a subordinate mediation that depends entirely upon the mediation of her Son.

Meditation

A form of prayer that includes silent reflection on a mystery of Christ as well as a quiet listening to what God wants to communicate, meditation in its many forms is a powerful means of spiritual growth. Meditative prayer is an essential counterpart to liturgical prayer and devotional exercises. Each type of prayer enriches the other. Gifts of meditative prayer from the Holy Spirit may raise the recipient to mystical contemplation, in which the person is granted unique ways to surrender to God's will.

Mercy

One of the grandest themes in all of Scripture is the mercy of God. The Father is "rich in mercy" (see Eph 2:4-5). Christ's parable of the Prodigal

Son celebrates the mercy of God (see Lk 15:11-32). Christ's defense of the woman taken in adultery is a striking example of how mercy and justice may work together (see Jn 8:3-11). The merciless treatment of millions of people in the twentieth century is a reminder of the need for bringing God's mercy to the world through works of human mercy. (For further study, see the encyclical *Rich in Mercy* by Pope John Paul II.) See also **Corporal Works of Mercy.**

Merit

The credit given to a person for an admirable act is the usual meaning of merit. But when the issue is between God and a human being, the meaning of merit has to be adjusted. Since people have received everything from God, the issue of merit must be based on the principle that God freely associates people with his grace.

God acts first. Human collaboration with God comes next. Whatever merit arises from these good works must first be attributed to God's grace. Then by God's gracious will humans are credited with merit for their good works.

The best prayer at this point is in the words of the psalmist: "Not to us, O Lord, not to us, but to your name give the glory" (Ps 115:1 NAB).

Messiah

Meaning "savior" or more literally "anointed one," the term *Messiah* is the Hebrew word translated into Greek as "Christ." It was applied to Jesus because in him was accomplished the divine mission signified by the title. Jesus was anointed by the Holy Spirit as king, priest, and prophet (see Lk 4:16-21).

Metanoia

The Greek word meaning "change of mind," *metanoia* is used in the New Testament to signify a conversion from sin to grace, from old ways to a commitment to Jesus Christ and his kingdom of salvation. It is not just a change of mind, but a change of heart, prompted by the Spirit and aided by grace.

Millennium

From the Latin meaning "a thousand years," the term refers to the thousand-year reign of Christ that appears six times in Revelation 20:2-7. St. Augustine interpreted this notion of a millennium to describe the era of the Church from Pentecost to the second coming of Jesus. The Church uses millennium in its calendar sense of dating the number of years since the birth of Christ. Hence the year 2000 was chosen to be a Jubilee of Christ's two-thousandth birthday. Strictly speaking, it should be 2001, but in popular usage the year 2000 was preferred.

Ministry

From the Latin for "service," ministry is properly applied to the service to the Church of ordained bishops, priests, and deacons. Broadly speaking, ministry has acquired a more extensive application to the various services of the lay faithful at liturgies and some other parish activities.

Miracles

Acts for which there are no human explanations and only divine ones are called miracles. Jesus performed mir-acles of healing and compassion such as giving sight to the blind, hearing to the deaf, and movement to the paralyzed. He raised the dead to life and expelled demons. He walked on the water, cursed a fig tree so that it withered, multiplied bread for five thousand people, and turned water into wine at Cana.

In the Gospels of St. Matthew, St. Mark, and St. Luke, Christ's miracles are both works of compassion and invitations to faith in him. In St. John's Gospel the miracles are called signs by which Jesus manifested his glory—or divinity. Miracles have continued to happen in the Church, and the process leading to canonization of a saint requires the authentication of miracles accomplished through the intercession of the candidate for sainthood.

Miraculous Medal

See **Immaculate Conception**.

Missionary Calling

By baptism all believers are called not just to practice the faith, but also to witness and share it with others. A good example of this calling is found in the story of the woman at the well (see Jn 4:4-42). After her conversion by Jesus, she returns to her village, proclaims Christ, and urges the people to come to him.

The very first recorded Christian sermon, given by St. Peter at Pentecost, is a missionary talk, announcing Christ's salvation and calling the listeners to faith and baptism. The missionary axiom is "Give faith to get faith," meaning that the dynamic growth in one's personal faith occurs when it is shared with others.

Miter

From the Greek *mitra,* meaning "turban," the miter is the liturgical hat worn by the pope and all other bishops of the Latin rite.

Mixed Marriages

When a Catholic marries a baptized non-Catholic, this is called a mixed marriage. Since the separation of Christians has not yet been overcome, the spouses can experience the problems of religious disunity within the family circle. Ecumenical dialogue has been pastorally helpful to such couples when they make the effort to live out their lives in the light of faith, reduce the tensions resulting from contrary obligations, encourage what is common to them in faith, and show respect for their differences.

Modernism

At the beginning of the twentieth century, a group of Catholic thinkers attempted to reconcile with Catholic doctrine the new thinking of the times in areas of Scripture, history, philosophy, and science. This modernizing of the faith (or modernism) was sometimes achieved at the expense of diluting doctrine or of compromising Church teachings in order to accommodate the new thinking. Pope St. Pius X condemned modernism in his decree *Lamentabili* and his encyclical *Pascendi*.

Monastery

A house for monks or cloistered nuns, a monastery can be a center of spirituality for the local area.

Monks

Men in consecrated life, monks live in community according to the evangelical counsels of poverty, chastity, and obedience. The best known monks are the Benedictines, who follow the Rule of St. Benedict.

Monogamy

The union of one man and one woman for a permanent marriage, monogamy is commanded by God, who is the author of marriage, as is made clear in Genesis 2:18-25.

Monotheism

The belief in one God, monotheism is the faith of Christians, Jews, and Muslims.

Monsignor

The designation "monsignor" is an honorary position bestowed on certain priests. A monsignor is part of the "papal household" and is able to wear a distinctive garb similar to bishops.

Monstrance

A gold vessel that contains a circular, glass-enclosed place for a large consecrated Host, the monstrance is used for exposition and benediction of the Blessed Sacrament. Its general shape is like a round, gold sunburst mounted on a vertical post with a base to sustain it. It is designed to draw people to honor and adore the Eucharist.

Mortal Sin

When an act destroys love in the human heart by the grave violation of God's law, a mortal sin has been committed. Such a sin turns a person away from God because the person has preferred a lesser good to God. For a mortal sin to be committed, three conditions must be present: grave matter, full knowledge of the evil of the act, and full consent of the will.

Still, it must be remembered that God's forgiving mercy is always present to the sinner. Jesus did not come to condemn people, but to save them (see Jn 3:17). People in mortal sin need encouragement to seek reconciliation with God and the Church in the sacrament of penance.

Mysteries of the Rosary

Every decade of the Rosary should be accompanied by a meditation on a scene in the life of Jesus or Mary. There are fifteen decades, divided into three sets of five mysteries: joyful, sorrowful, and glorious. The joyful mysteries are the Annunciation, Visitation, Birth of Christ, Presentation of the Lord, and Finding in the Temple. The sorrowful mysteries are the Agony in the Garden, Scourging at the Pillar, Crowning with Thorns, Carrying of the Cross, and Crucifixion. The glorious mysteries are the Resurrection, Ascension, Descent of the Holy Spirit, Assumption, and Crowning of Mary.

Mystical Body of Christ
See **Body of Christ.**

Natural Family Planning

A method of birth regulation, based on self-observation and the use of infertile periods in a woman's cycle, natural family planning is a morally acceptable act. The approach respects the bodies of the spouses and encourages communication and tenderness between them. For good reasons the spouses may wish to space the births of their children. Their desire should be based on a generosity appropriate to responsible parenthood (see *Catechism,* par. 2368, 2370).

Natural Law

The light of understanding placed in us by God, natural law enables us to know what good we should do and what evil we must avoid. The natural law is a reflection of the divine law made present in the consciousness of every human being. It is what gives every person a moral sense of what is good and bad, true and false, right and wrong. One of the greatest expressions of the natural law is found in the Ten Commandments.

Because of human sinfulness, the precepts of natural law are not always easily perceived. Grace and revelation are needed so that religious and moral truths may be seen more clearly.

Nature

Bearing several meanings, nature is first applied to the created world of earth and sky, mountains and seas, flowers and fruits of the earth. Nature also applies to animals and humans, that mysterious character that distinguishes one from the other. Human nature is understood in terms of the capacity to reason, choose, and imagine in a context of freedom. Despite its fallen state due to original sin, human nature can share by grace in the goodness and beauty of God's life.

Next, the term nature is applied to God. His divine nature or essence belongs to him alone. Each of the divine Persons possesses this divine nature. In addition, the Second Person of the Trinity assumed our human nature, uniting it to his divine nature, by being born of the blood and bone of the Virgin Mary.

Nave

Referring to the center aisle of a church that leads to the sanctuary and the altar, the term *nave* comes from a Latin word *navis,* meaning "ship." This name suggests the image of worshipers gathered in a divine ark or ship conveying them to God. The naves of the great Gothic cathedrals are noteworthy because of their soaring arches that come together like two hands folded in prayer. This inspirational architectural touch is meant to induce a prayerful attitude in the worshipers.

Nazorean (or Nazarene)

Because Jesus was raised in Nazareth and lived most of his life there, he was occasionally called a Nazorean (see Mt 2:23; Mk 16:6). The early Christians were sometimes referred to as a "sect of the Nazoreans" (see Acts 24:5).

New American Bible

An English translation of the Bible created by the members of the Catholic Biblical Association of America and sponsored by the Bishops' Committee of the Confraternity of Christian Doctrine. The New American Bible is based upon the original texts of the sacred books. With the approval of Church authority this translation was produced in cooperation with other Christian faiths so that all Christians might be able to use it.

New Covenant

A scriptural term denoting an agreement based on love between God and people, a covenant was first established between God and Israel (see Ex 19:2-6). It was a preparation for the gospel.

The New Covenant embraces all that is meant by what Jesus came to accom-

plish. His teachings, parables, miracles, example, selection, and formation of the twelve apostles and seventy-two disciples, redeeming death and resurrection, founding of the Church and sending of the Spirit, are the mighty acts of love that manifest his desire to covenant with the new people of God, the Church. The response of faith, with its active participation in the Church, sacraments and moral witness, completes the dynamic of the New Covenant.

New Testament

The twenty-seven books of the Bible written since the time of Christ, the New Testament includes the Gospels of Saints Matthew, Mark, Luke, and John. It also contains twenty-one epistles written by Saints Paul, Peter, James, John, and Jude, as well as the Acts of the Apostles and the Apocalypse (Revelation). Written in Greek, these books were most likely composed between A.D. 51 and 90.

Nicaea

Site of a palace of the emperor Constantine in the northeast corner of what is today Asiatic Turkey, Nicaea was selected to host two ecumenical councils. The first was held in 325 when the Church faced a denial of the divinity of Christ by Arius and his followers. The council reaffirmed the ancient faith of the Church in Christ's divinity and used

Greek philosophical terms such as "person" and "essence" to explain the scriptural truth about Christ as Son of God.

A second council was held at Nicaea in 787. It condemned iconoclasm and ordered the restoration of sacred images in churches. See also **Iconoclasm, Incarnation**.

Nicene Creed

Composed at the First Council of Nicaea in 325, the Nicene Creed emphasized the divinity of Christ. Because it did not mention the divinity of the Holy Spirit, some began to deny this truth of faith. The First Council of Constantinople in 381 responded to this denial by adding to the creed words about the Holy Spirit as Lord (God) and Giver of life who is to be worshiped and glorified. The Nicene Creed is normally the creed prayed at each Sunday liturgy.

Nihil Obstat

A Latin phrase meaning that "nothing stands in the way," the *nihil obstat* is a designation that must be given before a book receives an imprimatur, the Church permission for publication.

Nostra Aetate

The Vatican II constitution on the relationship of the Church to non-Christian religions, *Nostra Aetate* begins with a reflection on the Church's duty to foster unity and love between individuals, nations, and all peoples. The document notes the perennial questions about ultimate matters that have been addressed by the world's religions. Noting how Hinduism and Buddhism have approached these matters, the constitution gives special attention to the Muslim religion and pleads for renewed dialogue.

The largest portion of the document deals with Judaism, the "stock of Abraham." Besides outlining what is held in common by Jews and Christians, the Church states that "all Jews" who have lived, either at the time of Christ or today, may not be charged with Christ's death. The text adds that the Church deplores "all hatreds, persecutions, displays of anti-Semitism leveled at any time from any source against the Jews" (n. 4).

Notre Dame

French for "Our Lady," Notre Dame is the name given to many medieval French cathedrals, the most noteworthy being the one in Paris, as well as the University of Notre Dame in Indiana.

Novena

A consecutive nine-day set of public or private prayers offered in preparation for a Church feast such as Christmas or Pentecost, or in honor of the Virgin

Mary or another saint, a novena is a form of popular devotion. The practice began in the seventeenth century and took its inspiration from the nine days that Mary and the apostles spent in prayer to prepare for the coming of the Holy Spirit at Pentecost (see Acts 1:14; 2:1-4).

Novice

A new person enrolled in a religious order or congregation, a novice spends a year or more in intensive formation in prayer; growth in self-discipline and virtues; and study of the rules and traditions of the institute. This is a time for discerning the suitability of the candidate for consecrated life and the taking of first vows. The setting for novices is known as a novitiate, normally a place removed from the noise and distractions of everyday life.

Nun

Another name for a religious sister, committed to the consecrated life and the evangelical counsels of poverty, chastity, and obedience. Strictly speaking, religious women who take solemn vows are called nuns, while those taking simple vows are referred to as sisters.

Nuncio

A representative of the Holy See, the nuncio is a papal ambassador to those countries that have diplomatic relations with the Vatican. Besides his strictly diplomatic duties, the nuncio also keeps the pope informed about the state of the Church in the country where he is sent. In nations that do not maintain diplomatic relations with the Vatican, an Apostolic Delegate is appointed.

Nuptial Mass and Blessing

The liturgy at which spouses confer the sacrament of marriage on one another after the Gospel, the Nuptial Mass contains the Nuptial Blessing, which is given after the Our Father.

Old Testament

The Word of God as revealed to the People of Israel, the Old Testament is composed of the Law, the Prophets, the Histories, the Wisdom Books, and the Psalms. While there is great diversity in the authors, types of writing, stories, and number of centuries covered, the material is united by the theme of God's loving plan of salvation.

First the story is told of the creation of the world and of man and woman and their subsequent fall from grace in the first three chapters of Genesis. Then the remainder of the Old Testament is an account of God's gradual revelation of his inner life; his determination to establish a covenant people whose destiny was to witness to his true presence in the world; and his plan to send a Savior who would redeem them from sin and bring a new kingdom of grace. The forty-five books of the Old Testament contain unforgettable stories of courage and faith, sin and disobedience, divine mercy and compassion. The hopes of God's people in the Old Testament were finally realized in the birth, mission, and redemptive accomplishments of Jesus Christ.

Omnipotence, The Divine

To say that God is all-powerful is to acknowledge his omnipotence. Yet some object that since bad things happen to good people, God is not omnipotent. They believe God is all-good yet unable to overcome evil.

What they forget is the God-given gift of freedom people have, which can be misused and put at the service of evil. God is still omnipotent, but he will not override human freedom. God permits evil to happen. In fact, the Son of God endured the impact of evil, betrayal, and injustice in order to give us the graces needed to overcome evil.

Omniscience, The Divine

To acknowledge that God is all-knowing is to affirm his omniscience. Psalm 139 celebrates this quality of God. Some believe it means that God foresees what will happen to people, and so they are predetermined (or predestined) to a certain fate. Yet this is not the whole story.

People still have freedom and operate in an environment of unexpected circumstances. An omniscient God sees all this but does not determine the outcome like a puppeteer manipulating events. God permits human freedom to function, while providentially attempting to touch us with the prompting of the Holy Spirit to choose the good that is the true source of human fulfillment.

Oratory

Based on the Latin word for "prayer," the term *oratory* refers to a prayer room or chapel. St. Philip Neri set aside an oratory in his Roman residence, which he opened up for the study of Scripture, Church history, and spirituality, and for the fostering of ecclesial music as an instrument for catechesis. He engaged musicians such as Palestrina to compose music for scriptural stories. These compositions were performed in his oratory, thus inventing the name *oratorio* for such creations. The Order he founded became known as the Oratorians, of whom Cardinal Newman became one of its most celebrated members.

Ordinary

The ruling bishop of a diocese is called an ordinary inasmuch as he orders or administers the liturgical, spiritual, moral, pastoral, and apostolic life of the people, their priests, and their parishes, schools, hospitals, and other agencies.

Ordination

See **Holy Orders.**

Original Holiness

The condition of the first man and woman as described in the first three chapters of Genesis, original holiness refers to their state of unimpeded and graced orientation to God. Original sin deprived them of this holiness.

Original Sin

See **Sin, Original.**

Orthodox Church

Including all those Christians of Eastern churches who have valid sacraments and authentically ordained bishops, priests, and deacons, the Orthodox Church is separated from communion with the Catholic Church by reason of their rejection of the authority of the pope. They characterize themselves as orthodox believers who subscribe to true teachings in contrast to heterodox or heretical people who follow false teachings. The Orthodox Church formally separated from the Catholic Church in 1054. This separation is known in the West as the Eastern Schism.

In 1966 Pope Paul VI met with Ecumenical Patriarch Athenagoras in a symbolic gesture of reconciliation. Since then there has been an ongoing dialogue with the goal of the reunion of the two churches. Each year the Orthodox Church sends a delegation to St. Peter's basilica for the liturgy of Saints Peter and Paul. Conversely, the Catholic Church sends a delegation to the church of the ecumenical patriarch in Istanbul for the liturgy of St.

Andrew. In small but important ways the two churches are healing a thousand-year-old rift.

Our Lady

An affectionate title for the Virgin Mary, Our Lady (*Notre Dame* in French) is associated with almost every aspect of Catholic life and devotion.

Oxford Movement

The Anglican Church has historically experienced a tension between its Catholic origin and its Protestant development. It retained an attachment to the apostolic succession of bishops and the life of the sacraments. On the other hand it favored a Scripture-centered faith with emphasis on the role of the laity in church governance.

In the nineteenth century, a group of Anglican scholars at Oxford initiated a movement to recover the Catholic identity of their church. They published a series of tracts or research papers to this effect, especially using the writings of the fathers of the Church to support their approach. John Henry Newman became a leader of the effort and wrote Tract Ninety, which interpreted the "Thirty-Nine Articles" (the Anglican Reformation's dogmatic statement of Protestant principles) in a Catholic sense.

The controversy and opposition that this tract aroused caused Newman to examine his commitment to the Church of England. He decided that he must become a Catholic. He was reordained a Catholic priest and began a distinguished career as a Catholic theologian. Newman was named a cardinal in his old age and is said to have been a vital influence on the thinking of the theologians at Vatican II.

P

Pacifism

A theory that war can never be justified, Christian pacifism argues that all war is immoral and contrary to Christ's teachings (see Mt 5:39). Its proponents reject the Church's principles of "just war theory" and hold that a war using nuclear weapons is even more reprehensible. Pacifists believe that war cannot be conducted without an evil intention.

Paganism

Originally the name for polytheistic religions encountered by Christians in the Roman Empire, the term paganism eventually was used to describe non-Christian religions in mission lands. At the same time, it is not used for Judaism or the Muslim faith, nor for world religions such as Buddhism or Hinduism. By way of extension the extreme forms of modern secular society are sometimes referred to as pagan.

Pall

The white cloth placed over the coffin at Catholic funerals, the pall symbolizes the white robe the person wore at baptism. The journey of faith begun with this sacrament now concludes with the Mass of Christian Burial, fulfilling the promise of baptismal graces.

Pallium

A thin, triangular piece of white wool, stamped with six black crosses, the pallium is a symbol of elevation to the role of archbishop. Worn over the shoulders, the pallium is conferred by the pope on all new archbishops on the feast of Saints Peter and Paul, June 29.

Palm Sunday

The beginning of Holy Week, Palm Sunday celebrates the triumphal entry of Christ into Jerusalem on the eve of his passion and death. Palms are distributed to the worshipers. While the title of Palm Sunday remains the popular usage, the proper name of the day is Passion Sunday because it initiates the Church's direct reflection on the passion and one of the passion narratives from St. Matthew, St. Mark, or St. Luke is read.

Pantheism

A belief that in some way all people, places, and things are part of God, the term pantheism comes from the Greek, meaning all (*pan*) is God (*theos*). Certain aspects of contemporary New Age spirituality contain pantheistic tendencies. The problem with pantheism is its failure to distinguish between the

Creator and the creature. In its worst form it nourishes the pride that makes a god of oneself.

Papacy

The papacy encompasses the supreme jurisdiction and ministry of the pope as the universal pastor and shepherd of the whole Church. As the successor of St. Peter, the pope is the visible sign of the unity of faith and communion within the Church.

Papal Blessing

A blessing conveyed by the pope to an individual or a group either during a papal audience or liturgy or transmitted by a festive certificate, a papal blessing brings with it a plenary indulgence under the usual conditions. It may be given on other designated occasions, such as at a parish mission by a delegated priest.

Parable

Stories told by Jesus to illustrate a moral teaching or to probe the many-sided mystery of the kingdom of God, parables are a powerful means of communicating the gospel message. So memorable are parables such as the Good Samaritan and the Prodigal Son that they are widely recognized. The depths of their message and applicability have never been exhausted. The parable is more than a story designed to amuse or entertain. It is a Christ-given challenge to accept his kingdom of salvation, love, justice, and mercy.

Paraclete

From the Greek term meaning "advocate" or "lawyer," the word *paraclete* was used by Jesus to describe one of the major roles the Holy Spirit would exercise in the Church after his coming at Pentecost. The Holy Spirit would be the believers' advocate in our struggle to answer the call to holiness (see Jn 14:16-17). He will also be a "lawyer" in the sense that he will convict and convince people of their sinfulness—but also will convert them to life in Christ when they have repented and been open to his strong yet gentle action (see Jn 16:8).

Paradise

Referring to the Garden of Eden, which was the habitat of Adam and Eve as described in Genesis chapters one through three, the term *paradise* is also meant to describe the wonder and beauty of heaven through friendship and love with God. It was in this latter sense that Jesus promised salvation to the good thief at the cross (see Lk 23:43).

Parish

A stable community of the faithful within a diocese, the parish centered on the Eucharist and the other sacraments is the vital setting for the growth of faith, hope, love, and apostolic outreach.

Parochial Vicar

An associate pastor in a parish, the parochial vicar participates in the sacramental, pastoral, and administrative duties of a parish.

Parousia

The revelation of the glory of Christ at his second coming, the *parousia* will occur at the end of time. The event will be accompanied by the Last Judgment, the resurrection of the dead, and the appearance of the New Creation. It will be the time when creation and all of history reach their fulfillment.

Paschal Candle

The tall, ornamented festive candle blessed at the Easter Vigil, the paschal candle symbolizes the light of the risen Christ. It is given a prominent place in the sanctuary from Easter to Pentecost. It is also used for all funerals throughout the year to remind the mourners of the risen life in Christ promised to those who have been faithful to him on earth.

Paschal Mystery

Referring to the dynamic saving effect of Christ's death and resurrection, the paschal mystery is the central focus of Christianity. It is called paschal (from "passover") because of Christ's passing over from death to life. It is named a mystery since its truth can be grasped only by faith.

Passions

The emotions and feelings that incline people to good or evil, the passions include love and hate, fear and courage, anger, joy, and sadness. Because of the damage left over from original sin, the passions tend to rebel against right reason and discipline. For this reason people need to acquire virtues that restrain unruly passions and redirect them to positive goals of goodness.

Passover

The most solemn of Jewish feasts, the Passover recalls God's deliverance of the Jewish people from the avenging angel who slew the firstborn in Egypt and from the slavery they experienced in that land. The Passover celebrates the crossing of the Red Sea and the gifts of manna, quail, and water from the rock during their desert pilgrimage.

Its ceremonies are drawn from ancient agricultural feasts such as the wheat harvest, in which the first sheaves were offered to God and unleavened bread was eaten. Equally important was the harvest of the newborn lambs, the first of which was offered to God in thanksgiving. Finally, the grape harvest, yielding the new wine, also had an offering of the first fruits to God.

The lamb, bread, and wine became symbols by which the family at the Passover meal recalled the salvation deeds of God throughout their history. Jesus transformed the old Passover meal into the new one, the Eucharist, at the Last Supper.

Pastor

The priest who shepherds the parish as a servant-leader, the pastor celebrates the sacraments, provides pastoral care for the people, and oversees the necessary administrative tasks. He combines these three duties in his service as one who builds the parish into a community of faith, hope, love, and apostolic commitment.

Paten

The flat plate, usually a gold one, used to hold the consecrated host at Mass, the paten accompanies the chalice at every Eucharist.

Patriarch

In Scripture the patriarchs were the fathers of the first covenant generations, men such as Abraham, Isaac, Jacob, and Joseph. In Church hierarchy, patriarchs are bishops of ancient sees, especially in the Eastern Rite.

Patron Saints

The need for heavenly protectors and intercessors is met by the invocation of patron saints. In all kinds of ways patron saints are connected to the lives of believers, first with the giving of a saint's name at baptism and confirmation, then as patronal names for churches, dioceses, nations, schools, hospitals, seminaries, retreat houses, abbeys, monasteries, convents, and numerous other institutions of the Church. These canonized friends of God are also friends of believers on earth in the loving communion of saints.

Paul, St.

Born an observant Jew at Tarsus, St. Paul studied under Gamaliel in Jerusalem to become a rabbi. Fluent in Latin, Greek, and Hebrew and designated a Roman citizen because of his birth in Tarsus, St. Paul brought a wealth of talent to his ministry. As a fervent rabbinic Jew he was opposed to the new Christian movement, which he perceived as departing from the ancient faith. He approved the martyrdom of St. Stephen.

While on a journey to Damascus to arrest Christians, however, he was struck by a blinding light and given a direct experience of Christ, who called him to conversion. St. Paul was baptized, and after a time of reflection on his spiritual experience he began preaching Christ. He sensed that he was called to preach the gospel to the Gentiles, in which ministry he realized that it was not necessary for them to be circumcised or to follow Jewish dietary laws in order to be Christians. His position was vindicated at the Council of Jerusalem (see Acts 15).

Inspired by the Spirit, St. Paul took the gospel to Europe in several missionary journeys. He established churches in places such as Corinth, Philippi, and Thessalonica. He kept in touch with his mission churches with epistles that became part of the New Testament. His final days were spent in Rome under house arrest, and he was martyred by the emperor Nero around A.D. 62.

Peace, Exchange of

After the Our Father and just before Communion comes an exchange of peace among the worshipers at Mass. Normally this is done by shaking hands and greeting each other with words of peace in Christ. The ritual remembers Christ's gift of peace to his apostles at the Last Supper.

Pectoral Cross

Worn over the shoulders by bishops and abbots, the pectoral cross is attached to a chain and rests on the chest. It is a visible sign of their unity with the cross of Christ and their commitment to the sacrificial love needed to bring salvation to others.

Penance

Initially an internal conversion of the heart away from sin and towards God, penance is a graced movement of the soul that signals a change of heart in one's life. Penance is also an external act by which the interior conversion event is expressed and strengthened. The principal forms of external penance are prayer, fasting, and charitable giving.

Penance, Sacrament of

See **Reconciliation, Sacrament of**.

Penitent

The sinner who repents of sin and seeks forgiveness is the penitent who goes to the sacrament of reconciliation with a contrite heart and a willingness to confess sins and make satisfaction for them.

Pentateuch

The first five books of the Bible, the Pentateuch consists of Genesis, Exodus, Leviticus, Numbers, and Deuteronomy. These books constitute the Law or the Torah of the Old Testament. They contain the accounts of creation and the fall of our first parents, the promise of redemption, and God's creation of a covenant people. These covenant people are called to witness to the true God in a polytheistic world of idolatry.

Leviticus outlines the seriousness with which the people took their call to worship God with reverence and care. Deuteronomy expands the application of the Ten Commandments to everyday life and illustrates the moral awareness developed by God's people. Jesus took his two laws of love from these two books of the Pentateuch: love of God (from Dt 6:4-5) and love of neighbor (from Lv 19:18).

Pentecost

Originally a Jewish feast observed fifty days after Passover, Pentecost celebrated the grape harvest and the giving of the covenant at Sinai. Pentecost became a Christian celebration because of the descent of the Holy Spirit upon the one hundred and twelve disciples in the Upper Room fifty days after Easter. At this first Pentecost after the resurrection and ascension of Jesus, the Holy Spirit was manifested as a divine Person to the Church sent to fulfill the paschal mystery of Christ as he had promised.

At the same time on this feast, the Holy Spirit manifested the Church to the world. St. Peter's first sermon explained the meaning of the event and called the listeners to conversion to Christ and baptism, with the result that three thousand converts were made. Hence the Spirit's action is connected to evangelization, sharing faith and inviting others to become followers of Christ as members of the Church.

People of God

The founding of the first covenant people of God, Israel, was done at God's initiative. The Hebrew word for God's people is *qahal*, meaning a "called community." Jesus Christ founded the second called community, the Church, as God's people destined to be a sacrament of salvation for the world. It is important to stress God's initiative in this process because it must be held that the community did not come into existence by the consent of the governed, but only by God's gracious will. In the Church, Christ instituted a new and eternal covenant by which a new priestly, prophetic, and royal people of God share in these offices of Christ and the mission this implies for the world.

Perjury

The making of a false statement under oath, perjury also occurs when one makes a promise under oath with no intention of keeping it. Perjury violates the second and eighth commandments.

Perpetual Adoration

The devotional practice of perpetual adoration of the Blessed Sacrament is the vocation of certain religious congregations and a commitment frequently made by parishes. In the latter case a team of volunteers pledge to take an hour of adoration so that in the course of a week, every hour is covered. The Blessed Sacrament is exposed in a monstrance. The practice appears in modified form in holy hours, adoration from 9 A.M. to 5 P.M., and the Forty Hours devotion.

In all its forms this devotion has become more popular in recent times because the faith in Christ's real presence has declined and also because the need for reparation for the violence and sin in the world is more apparent. Another reason is that this hour of restful prayer nourishes a contemplative spirit. Not only does Christ seem to come closer to people, but the people feel nearer to Christ.

Person, Divine

From the word *hypostasis* in Greek, the term *person* is applied to the Father, to the Son, and to the Holy Spirit. Each divine person is related to the other two, but distinct from them, while being united in one divine nature in the Trinity. Hence there are three divine persons in one God.

Person, Human

Made in the image and likeness of God, the human person has a mind that can know the truth, a will that can love the good, and an identity that is utterly unique. A human person is not something, but someone. Capable of being a person in communion, human persons can form bonds of community with God and each other for the sake of the common good and mutual support. In fact a human person needs to live in society bound together by a principle of unity that transcends each one.

Peter, St.

Established by Christ as the chief of the apostles, St. Peter was a Galilean fisherman called to be an apostle together with his brother St. Andrew. He is the first apostle to confess Jesus to be Christ, the Son of the living God (see Mt 16:16-19). Jesus praised him for this confession and changed his name from Simon to Peter (or the Rock) upon which he would build the Church.

Blustery, impulsive, and loyal, St. Peter also proved to be a coward during the passion, when he denied Christ three times. Yet he immediately repented and wept tears of sorrow. The risen Jesus gave him the public opportunity to reverse his denial with three affirmations of love.

The New Testament mentions St. Peter more times than all the other apostles put together. He has a "firstness" about him that dramatizes his leadership in the Church. He gives the first sermon at Pentecost, converts the first Gentile, Cornelius, and becomes the first bishop of Antioch, the first diocese outside of the Holy Land.

When he went to Rome he became its bishop, and the popes, his successors, are bishops of Rome. Along with St. Paul he was martyred in Rome in the persecution of Nero about A.D. 62.

Peter's Pence

An annual collection taken up to help finance the work of the Holy See, Peter's Pence gets its name from the origin of the collection in the eighth century when one penny per person was requested.

Pharisees

Jewish religious leaders in late Old Testament times, the Pharisees were custodians of tradition and observance of the Torah or Law. Their disciplined interpretation of their faith did much to preserve the faith and identity of God's people during several centuries of turmoil and chaos preceding Christ's time. While it was clear that some of them erred on the side of hypocrisy and burdened people's consciences—as Christ illustrated in his criticisms—yet in general they were good men. A number of Pharisees opposed Christ, but at the same time the New Testament praises the Pharisees Nicodemus and Gamaliel (see Jn 3:1-21; 7:45-48; Acts 5:34).

Piety

One of the seven gifts of the Holy Spirit, piety inclines people to be devoted to God. It is also a virtue associated with filial attention and loyalty to one's parents and family. A third meaning of piety refers to acts of popular religious devotion that have always been a valued expression of the faith.

Pilgrim, Pilgrimage

A journey to a shrine of Christ, Mary, or a saint, a pilgrimage is a spiritual voyage meant to deepen the faith of the pilgrim. Since the life of faith itself is often described as a pilgrimage, it is appropriate that this be symbolized by an actual journey. Frequently people go to shrines to seek various kinds of healing: physical, emotional, and spiritual. The most-frequented pilgrimage sites include Jerusalem, Rome, Lourdes, Guadalupe, and Czestechowa. Spiritual benefits such as plenary indulgences are given to pilgrims. Holy Years are special times for pilgrimages.

Polygamy

The practice of having more than one wife at the same time, polygamy is contrary to the unity of one man and woman in a marriage and offends against the dignity of the woman.

Pope

See **Holy Father.**

Poverty, Vow of

Men and women committed to the consecrated life take the vow of poverty, in which they voluntarily renounce the ownership of property or money. This holding of all they own in common is essential for the true community life that consecrated life demands. It reflects the fulfillment of the first beatitude about poverty of spirit (see Mt 5:3) and echoes the ideal of gospel life as seen in the description of the first Christian community in the Acts of the Apostles (see Acts 4:44-45).

Prayer

The act whereby people of faith raise their minds and hearts to God to express praise and adoration, to thank the Lord for gifts received, and to ask for blessings needed. The liturgy of the Church as found in the Eucharist and the other sacraments is the most important form of prayer. Allied to this is the Liturgy of the Hours, where people pray in psalms and hymns and meditatively recite readings from Scripture and other sacred writers.

For every believer there are three expressions of prayer: vocal prayer, meditation, and contemplation. These forms correspond to the invocation: "May the Lord be on my lips, in my mind, and in my heart." Vocal prayer involves our voice and physical acts. Since the Word became flesh to speak to us, it is fitting that our words become flesh in order to speak to Christ. The Rosary is an outstanding and powerful vocal prayer.

Meditation calls on the mind to attend to God and seek what the Lord asks of us. Books help people meditate, especially the writings of Scripture, the Church fathers, and great spiritual masters. One may also read the "books" of creation and history to discern God's active presence there. There are many methods of meditation, with each method a different means to reach the same goal of encountering Jesus.

Contemplation is prayer of the heart. It is part of the simplifying of prayer life from many words and numerous thoughts to "resting" in Jesus. We look at Jesus and Jesus looks at us. This requires us to give time to be alone with him in peaceful solitude. The *Catechism* (par. 2709-19) gives excellent direction for this form of prayer.

Prayer of the Faithful

In every liturgy just before the offering of the gifts, the prayer of the faithful is recited. The people pray for the graces needed by the pope and bishops and other leaders, along with communal and personal needs arising at a given moment.

Preaching

After the Gospel at Mass the priest or deacon preaches a homily that explains the doctrinal and moral meaning of the Word of God and relates it to the lives of the worshipers. This ministry of the Word is an essential aspect of our faith inasmuch as God's revelation and doctrinal reflection upon it are meant to be heard, interpreted, and applied to Christian living.

It is important that the preacher be a witness to what is said in the Scripture. The credibility of a homily is strengthened by the evident faith and example of the preacher. Pope Paul VI taught that people today listen only to witnesses, and that if they listen with acceptance to a homilist, it is because the preacher is already a witness. (For further study read *Evangelii Nuntiandi* by Pope Paul VI.)

Prelate

A title related to those who have a role in the hierarchy of the Church, the term prelate is applied to the pope and all bishops, abbots, and certain other authority figures in the Church. It is also an honorary title held by monsignors.

Presbyter

Meaning "elder," the title presbyter appears often in the New Testament and is associated with the priesthood.

As the Church developed after the apostles died, the successors to the apostles were named bishops as overseers of the Church. They in turn ordained presbyters (priests) and deacons to help with the sacramental, pastoral, and administrative needs of the Church. While some New Testament descriptions of bishops and presbyters as overseers were interchangeable at first, the distinctions between bishop and presbyter-priest became fixed and clear by the year 110, when the title of bishop was restricted to the leader of the presbyters.

Presentation of the Lord

St. Joseph and Mary brought the baby Jesus to the temple to present him to God according to the Law of Moses. Tradition held that the firstborn son should be offered to God, symbolized by the offering of the turtledoves in this case. This presentation of the Lord was witnessed by St. Simeon and St. Anna. They received the gift of seeing in this Child both the fulfillment of the messianic hope of Israel and a sign of contradiction (see Lk 2:22-39).

Presumption

An act or attitude opposed to the virtue of hope, presumption assumes that trust in oneself is sufficient for salvation. It can also refer to the assumption that one can be saved regardless of one's behavior, due to a misunderstanding of divine mercy.

Pride

One of the seven capital sins, pride is the result of arrogant self-confidence that excludes dependence on God as well as a proper sense of communion with others. It results in power-seeking competition with others, a vain desire for notice, and a rivalry with God.

Priest

See **Holy Orders**.

Priesthood of Christ

The real high priest in the line of Melchizedek, Jesus Christ fulfilled all that was signified by the Old Testament priesthood (see Heb 5:10; 6:20). While previous priests offered sacrificial victims of bulls and lambs, Jesus offered himself as the ultimate victim to attain our salvation (see Heb 10:14). Christ's priesthood is made present in the Church through the ministerial priesthood conferred in holy orders.

Priesthood of the Faithful

See **Laity**.

Primacy of the Pope

See **Holy Father**.

Primate

A title of honor, the name is given to the bishop of the oldest diocese in a given country.

Private Revelation

Special revelations confided to certain persons throughout Church history after the end of apostolic times. Private revelation has the principal value of illumining and defending public revelation as passed on in Apostolic Tradition and Scripture and interpreted by the Magisterium. Private revelation is designed to help people live their faith more completely. Some private revelations have been recognized by Church authority. Others, which claim to surpass or correct the revelation of Christ confided to the Church, have been rejected.

Profession of Faith

The expression of belief in what Catholics believe, the profession of faith is offered in the words of the Nicene and Apostles' Creeds.

Profession, Religious

The religious profession commits the person to live the evangelical counsels expressed in the vows of poverty, chastity, and obedience taken by the members of consecrated life. Normally, there are two stages in such a profession, the first occurring after a novitiate and called simple vows, and the second being made a few years later in final vows—sometimes called solemn vows. This public taking of vows and the approval by the Church as well as the religious institute indicate the seriousness of the act and a corresponding commitment to live the vows.

Propagation of the Faith, Society for the

An international organization set up by the Church to collect funds for the support of the missions, the Society for the Propagation of the Faith has national offices in countries where the collections are taken. Distribution to mission lands is awarded according to need. A collection of this kind takes place once a year in each parish.

Prophet

Called by God to form God's people in the ways of the covenant, the prophets interpreted for them the signs of the times in the light of God's word, taught them correct moral behavior, and awakened in them messianic hopes. Many of them wrote books that became part of God's revealed word in the Old Testament. St. John the Baptist concluded the prophetic work of the Old Testament.

Protestant

Begun by the Reformation when Martin Luther protested the abuse of indulgences by the Church, the Protestant denominations began by separating themselves from Catholicism. They took differing shapes: Lutheran in Germany and Scandinavia; Anglican in England; Calvinist/Presbyterian in Switzerland and Scotland. Subsequently, numerous other Protestant denominations were founded.

In general, a Protestant is a baptized Christian (other than a member of one of the Eastern Churches) who believes in Christ and does not accept Catholic faith in its entirety but has received the gift of the Holy Spirit and grace. The ecumenical movement is designed to bring about the unity of all baptized Christians.

Proto-Evangelium

Known as the "first Gospel," the *proto-evangelium* is the good news mysteriously promised by God to Eve that a Messiah and Redeemer would come to correct the effects of the first sin (see Gn 3:15).

Providence

The mysterious influence that God exercises within creation to guide it to its intended fulfillment, God's providence shows that he did not abandon the world after creating it. God has remained with the processes of creation to protect, guide, and sustain it and all that dwell therein.

Prudence

The virtue that inclines a person to discern what is good and choose it, prudence is one of the cardinal virtues. Since such an insight often must cope with extremes and conflicting tensions, this virtue was called the "charioteer of the virtues" by St. Thomas Aquinas. Prudence moves the Christian to live by the law of Christ and provides the immediate guidance for the judgment of conscience.

Psalms, Book of

The prayer book of the Old Testament, the book of Psalms (150 of them) was assembled over several centuries. This collection of prayers in the form of hymns, canticles, and poetry has been used since the time of Christ in the public prayer of the Church, especially in every Eucharist and the Liturgy of the Hours. Along with the Gospels, no other book of the Bible is used more frequently.

The psalms are meant to be sung, and over the centuries various chants and other types of music have been composed to make this possible. Since they are sung to translated texts, the original rhythms of the Hebrew need to be transposed, a challenge not easy to achieve. The important point to remember is that this book of prayers is inspired by God to give believers examples of praise, petition, thanksgiving, lament, complaint, suffering, joy, and adoration to suit the many movements of the soul in its communications with God.

Punishment, Eternal

The penalty for an unrepented mortal sin, eternal punishment separates the sinner from communion with God forever. The sinner goes to hell for all eternity.

Punishment, Temporal

The temporal punishment due to sin completes the cleansing of the soul to prepare it for eternal communion with God in heaven by the purification of an unwholesome attachment to creatures, even after death. This purification of the soul is begun on earth by prayer, fasting, charitable giving, and moral discipline. If not completed before death, it is finished in purgatory.

Purgatory

A state of final purification after death for those who died in God's friendship but are not totally free of attachment to creatures. Purgatory cleanses the soul of remaining imperfections and prepares the person to enter into final communion with God in heaven.

Q Document

From the German word *Quelle,* meaning "source," the Q document is a hypothetical text that Scripture scholars have posited to explain the similarities found in the Gospels of St. Mark, St. Matthew, and St. Luke. C.H. Weisse developed the concept in 1838. According to this theory, there were a series of sayings and other small units from the life, preaching, and ministry of Jesus that were written down in Q. In turn, this material was taken by St. Mark and formed into the first Gospel, which then became a major influence in the writing of St. Matthew and St. Luke.

The hypothesis became popular first among Protestant Scripture scholars and later among Catholic ones, but a smaller group of scholars in both camps rejects the theory. No Q text has ever been found, and the solution to Gospel similarities and differences can be explained without it.

Queenship of Mary

A feast created by Pope Pius XII in the Marian Year of 1950, the Queenship of Mary is celebrated on August 22, eight days after the celebration of Mary's Assumption into heaven. Mary is declared Queen of angels and saints, both in heaven and on earth.

Rabbi

A Hebrew word that means both "teacher" and "master," the term *rabbi* was often used by the apostles when they addressed Jesus. He was more than a teacher who would instruct them. He was their master, who lived what he taught and expected them to be more than students learning a lesson, but rather disciples who practiced and witnessed to what they were taught.

Rapture

Generally a description of ecstasy caused either by romantic love or by a spiritual experience, the term *rapture* has acquired a specific meaning among people with millenarian beliefs. These Christians hold that Jesus will come in the clouds in the last period of history and gather up, or *rapture*, the true believers into the heavens. In heaven they will be prepared to rule with Christ during a thousand years of peace on earth—a millennium. This view is based on their interpretation of 1 Thessalonians 4:16-17 and Matthew 24:29-44 as a rapture scene and linked with the millennium texts of Revelation 20:1-6.

The Church's view of the Thessalonian text is that it refers to Christ's parousia and the resurrection of the dead. The Church follows St. Augustine's interpretation of the millennium verses of the book of Revelation, which holds that the text speaks of the era of the Church from Pentecost to the second coming of Christ. In St. Matthew, Christ's judgment sermon predicts the second coming of the Son of Man and concludes with practical advice on how to be vigilant and prepared. These virtues of watchfulness apply to the everyday life of Christians as well as to one's eventual death, while also referring to preparation for Christ's second coming.

Rash Judgment

A baseless evaluation of someone's behavior or words, rash judgment is an unfair assessment of another person. It is a sin against the virtue of justice. Jesus spoke against rash judgment in Matthew 7:1-2. On the other hand, proper judgments— reasoned, charitable, and based on facts—can and should be made.

Readings, Cycle of

The scriptural readings assigned for the liturgy are found in the lectionary and arranged into a three-year cycle: A, B, C. The synoptic Gospels are thus spread out into the year of St. Matthew, the year of St. Mark, and the year of St.

Luke. St. John's Gospel is read every year on Good Friday and at Easter time. In a similar way the Old Testament and readings from Acts, the Epistles, and Revelation are parceled out in such a way that major portions of these books will be read and heard over three years.

Real Presence

There are degrees of Christ's presence, particularly as seen at the liturgy. Christ is present in the priest who presides, in the assembly of the worshipers, in the scriptural word that is proclaimed, and by the symbolism of the altar. But there is a greater and unique presence of Jesus Christ in the consecrated bread and wine of the Eucharist, where he is present by his Body, Blood, Soul, and Divinity.

This is the Church's faith in his real presence. Believers deepen their faith in the real presence by adoration and Communion at Mass and by adoration of the reserved Presence in the tabernacle outside of Mass (see *Catechism*, par. 1378-79).

Reconciliation, Sacrament of

Since sin divides people from God, each other, and the Church, a divine forgiveness is necessary to remove the sin and reconcile the sinners with everyone from whom they are alienated. Christ's redeeming work has achieved this reconciliation and made it available in the Church through the sacrament of reconciliation.

Rector

A priest who is in charge of a cathedral or a seminary is called a rector.

Red Mass

A Mass held to seek divine guidance for judges and lawyers, the Red Mass is so called because it is the Mass of the Holy Spirit, in which red vestments are used.

Redemption

Another word for salvation, the term *redemption* describes the act by which Jesus Christ saved people from their sins and obtained divine life for them. The whole of Christ's life—from his incarnation in the womb of Mary to all the mysteries of his teachings, witness, death, resurrection, and sending of the Spirit to abide with the Church—comprise the totality of his redemptive act.

Reformation

See **Protestant**.

Reign of God

See **Kingdom of God**.

Relativism

A philosophical position which holds that truth cannot be known, relativism concludes that there can only be opinions, not the certainty of absolute truths. This philosophy prevails in contemporary culture, especially in the area of morality.

Relics

In Catholic tradition, relics are the deceased bodies of saints, or parts of such bodies, or pieces of cloth or other items that have been touched to the bodies of saints. These relics are held up as objects of veneration for the faithful, inviting the believers to invoke the intercession of the given saint for their needs. The tradition goes back to the early Church, when honor of this kind was given to the bodies of martyrs such as St. Polycarp (d. 156).

Religion

Popularly, the term *religion* refers to one's denominational affiliation or to one of the world's non-Christian systems of belief and practice. For Catholics, religion is also a virtue that binds a person to God in acts of worship, obedience, and commitment. The first three of the Ten Commandments are expressions of the virtue of religion.

Reparation

By his sacrifice on the cross, Jesus made amends, or a reparation, for the sins of all people. After every confession the forgiven sinner is expected to make a suitable reparation for offenses against God and others. This is particularly true in the case of sins against truth and justice, in which the penitent must correct the harm done to another's good name and make restitution of stolen goods.

Repentance

See **Penance**.

Requiem

For many years, the word *requiem* meant a Mass for the dead or a general remembrance service for a deceased person. Since Catholics today speak of the Mass of Christian Burial, the term *requiem* is declining in common usage.

Reredos

An altarpiece consisting of statuary or other artwork constructed behind an altar, the reredos was common when altars were built against the back wall of the Church and the priest faced the wall when Mass was celebrated. With the arrival of free-standing altars and the priest's facing the people for Mass, the role of the reredos has less prominence. At the same time, many are artistic masterpieces.

Resurrection of the Body

In both the Nicene and Apostles' Creeds the faithful express their belief in the resurrection of the body that will occur when Jesus Christ comes again to judge the living and the dead. In the present state, when people die, their souls survive while the body decays. Because of the resurrection of Christ's body, however, all human bodies will rise again. Soul and body will be united so that the whole person rises from the dead. This teaching

is clearly stated by St. Paul in
1 Corinthians chapter fifteen.

Resurrection of Christ

Christ's resurrected body is real flesh
that can be touched and seen. The risen
Jesus was able to eat a meal and discuss
matters with his apostles and disciples.
He was not a ghost. At the same time,
Christ's body had transcendent, mysterious powers, such as the ability to walk
through closed doors and not be
restrained by time and space.

St. Paul argued that Christ's resurrection was so essential to Christian
teaching and belief that if it did not
happen, then faith is vain and useless
(see 1 Cor 15:14). Together with
Christ's crucifixion and death, his resurrection forms one unified act of salvation, providing death to sin and the
treasure of divine life for all people who
come in faith to Christ and the Church.

Retreat

A spiritual exercise that involves voluntary cessation of workaday actions and a
special commitment to prayer, silence,
and reflection, a retreat is a temporary
withdrawal from normal activities in
order to get in touch with God and to
experience spiritual renewal. Retreats
can be as short as a day and as long as a
month; the Ignatian Exercises, for
example, are also known as the Thirty-
Day Retreat. The pace of modern life,

and the numerous distractions that
accompany it, tends to weaken the spiritual appetite and take the fervor out of
faith. A retreat is designed to counter
spiritual ennui, energize faith, and
enliven one's personal relationship
with Christ.

Revelation

The First Vatican Council taught that
human reason can arrive at the existence of God. But it also noted that
there are truths about the inner life of
God and the divine plan of salvation
that can only be known if God tells us.
This is the meaning of revelation that is
God's gracious self-disclosure of his
intimate life in the Trinity and the loving plan to save us in the redemptive
acts of Jesus Christ.

Revelation was first communicated
to the ancient patriarchs, prophets, and
men of wisdom. Revelation was completely contained in Jesus Christ, the
living Word of God made flesh.
Revelation is found in Apostolic
Tradition, the books of the Bible, and
the living tradition of the worshiping
and witnessing Church led and interpreted by the Magisterium of the popes
and bishops.

Revelation, Book of

The last book of Scripture, the book of
Revelation (also called the Apocalypse, a
word that means "revelation") was

originally written to strengthen the faith and courage of Christians facing Roman persecution. But as the Word of God, it speaks to the Church of every age, especially during recurrent persecutions that require a response of courageous witness in the face of such trials. This book is filled with symbolic language—with the exception of chapters two and three—borrowed from numerous references to Old Testament prophecies.

While there is much about tribulations to be experienced, there is more about the victory of the risen Christ and the triumphant hymns of the elect in the heavenly liturgies. So, despite the trials described, Revelation is a book of Christian hope. The final chapters describe the mysterious transformation of the world into the new creation by the power of Jesus Christ.

Right to Die

There is no right to die if this means that explicit means can be taken to end a human life, such as is the case in euthanasia and physician-assisted suicide. At the same time, one is not required to use extraordinary means to stay alive in the case of a life-threatening illness. On the other hand, one should take advantage of treatments that are inexpensive, effective, and not burdensome. Pain management is recommended so long as there is no direct intention to kill the patient.

Right to Life

Everyone has the right to life, especially those who are weak and defenseless, such as the unborn, people with disabilities, civilians in war zones, the elderly sick, and the terminally ill. A consistent life ethic defends human life from the womb to the tomb. God is the author of life and has given the world the fifth commandment, which forbids murder and upholds the sanctity of life.

Rite of Christian Initiation of Adults

See **Catechumens**.

Rites

Throughout history various liturgical traditions have emerged in which the one Catholic and apostolic faith is expressed and celebrated in different cultures and countries. In the West the Roman or Latin rite prevails. In the East are the Byzantine, Coptic (Alexandrian), Syrian, Armenian, and Chaldean rites. The words *rite* and *ritual* are often used interchangeably.

Roman Catholic

Acts 11:26 reports that the disciples of Christ were first called Christians in the city of Antioch. Later, the third bishop of Antioch, St. Ignatius (A.D. 30–107), was the first one to refer to the Church as "Catholic" or universal (see *Letter to the Smyrnaeans*, 8:20). Since the

Reformation in the sixteenth century, the custom arose of calling Christians in union with the bishop of Rome "Roman Catholics." At first this had a negative connotation because of the division of Christians, but today the title is simply common usage.

Rosary

Commonly prayed using a circle of beads with five sets of ten (each called a decade) separated by a single bead, the Rosary honors the Blessed Virgin Mary. It includes meditations on the mysteries of Christ's life, from his incarnation to his ascension, and the life of Mary. Each decade begins with the statement of the designated mystery and the recitation of the Our Father. This prayer is followed by ten Hail Marys, during which time the person reflects on the mystery. The decade closes with the Glory Be to the Father. The Rosary was developed by people in the Middle Ages as a popular prayer that substituted for the Liturgy of the Hours.

Rubrics

Referring to rules for the proper celebration of the liturgy, the term *rubrics* comes from the Latin for "red," the color in which the rules are printed in the various books used for liturgical celebrations.

S

Sabbath

The name given to the seventh day of the Hebrew week, the word Sabbath also means "rest." It commemorates the seventh day on which the Lord rested after the six days of creation (see Gn 2:2-3). The Jewish observance of the Sabbath remembers God's creative work and continuing providence today. It also recalls God's initiative in calling the Jewish people to a covenant with him.

Christianity continues the observance of the Sabbath, but it is moved to Sunday in memory of the Lord's resurrection from the dead. The Sunday Sabbath observance is a time for worshiping God at the Eucharist and relaxing from the demands of work.

Sacrament

A sacrament is an outward sign, instituted by Christ and entrusted to the Church for the purpose of imparting grace and divine life. There are sacraments of initiation: baptism, confirmation, the Eucharist; sacraments of healing: reconciliation and anointing; and sacraments of communion: matrimony and holy orders. The Church is the sacrament of salvation, the institution and community by which the Holy Spirit brings the saving power of Christ

to bear on those who are open to his redemptive graces.

Sacramental

A sacramental is a sign that resembles a sacrament. It may be an act, such as the sign of the cross or the sprinkling of holy water, usually accompanied by a prayer. It may also be an object, such as a crucifix or Rosary.

Sacramentals prepare people to receive the full benefit of sacraments and they sanctify the different circumstances of life. Many of the sacramentals involve a blessing such as that a parent may give a child. Sacramentals are part of popular piety, which takes distinctive forms depending on local custom and culture.

Sacraments of Initiation

See **Catechumens**.

Sacred

The realm of the holy, the sacred carries the divine presence into the midst of everyday life. Acts of blessing and consecration are ways in which the created world is consciously united to God and able to reflect the sense of the sacred.

Sacred Heart Devotion

Designed to help people get in touch with divine mercy and love, the devotion to the Sacred Heart of Jesus was promoted by St. Margaret Mary Alacoque. Her visions of Christ from 1673 to 1675 led her to advance this focus on Christ's mercy and love in a time when there was an excess of fear and guilt in religious practice. This devotion brought about a balance in the approach to God's justice and mercy, a corrective of love where there was too much fear, and a vision of forgiveness to address the guilt of sin.

The devotion has had a sturdy life in the Church, enduring to the present day. A feast of the Sacred Heart is celebrated on the Friday after the feast of Corpus Christi. Many perceive St. Faustina's visions of Christ's divine mercy as a contemporary renewal and continuance of St. Margaret Mary's contribution to the faith life of Catholics.

Sacrifice

From the Latin meaning "to make holy," the term *sacrifice* refers to a form of worship that is recorded in the earliest pages of Scripture as seen in the story of Cain and Abel (see Gn 4:3-6). There were five forms of sacrifice in the Old Testament.

A *holocaust* transformed the offering (usually a lamb or a bull) in a fire that consumed it and sent all of the gift to God. The holocaust expressed absolute dependence on God. A second type of sacrifice was the *libation* or wine-pouring ceremony. A bowl of new wine was poured over a rock so it could seep into the ground and thus be symbolically given to God, often in appreciation for the grape harvest. The ceremony "toasted" God for his generosity.

The third form of sacrifice was the *bread offering.* Twelve wheat loaves were placed on a gold table in the temple every seven days. Incense burned in front of the loaves, symbolizing the offering of this food to God in thanksgiving for his providence.

Similar to this was the fourth sacrifice, the *wheat offering,* at the end of the wheat harvest. Sheaves of new wheat were waved over the altar and consumed with a loaf of new bread in fire to praise God for the harvest.

Finally, the *friendship* meal—or Passover meal—was the most solemn of sacrifices, since it included a piece of a sacrificed lamb as well as unleavened bread. The meal celebrated Israel's liberation from Egypt and the covenant God made with them, both through the patriarchs and at Sinai.

Christ's sacrifice at the cross gathered up these five forms of sacrifice and brought them to fulfillment as the ultimate new covenant and the act that saved the world from sin. The Holy

Eucharist continues Christ's sacrifice and all that it means.

Sacrifice of the Mass

The Mass is a sacrifice inasmuch as it makes present in a sacramental and unbloody manner the sacrifice of Jesus Christ at the cross. This is a mystery of faith that reveals to us the generosity of Christ in making available through the Holy Eucharist his ultimate saving act at Calvary at each Mass. Hence the graces of the cross become available to the faithful at every Eucharist.

Through the ministry of the ordained priest, Christ makes it possible for the members of the Christian assembly to offer the Father a perfect sacrifice that is Christ himself, pleasing in every way and able to bring forth countless blessings. Moreover, just as Christ at Calvary fulfilled all five forms of Old Testament sacrifice, so in the Mass are all these types of sacrifice available to us in their final meaning because of Christ.

Sacrilege

The abusive desecration of what is holy, a sacrilege is an act of profound disrespect for persons, places, or things dedicated to God's service. A sacrilege is a serious sin when it profanes or abuses the Eucharist because in this sacrament the Body of Christ is substantially present for us.

Sacristan

The person who looks after the vessels, vestments, and books related to the liturgy, a sacristan assists the priest and others involved in worship by preparing all that is necessary for the service.

Sadducees

A small group of educated and prosperous men, the Sadducees served as part of the religious leadership of the Jewish community at the time of Christ. They confined their beliefs to the doctrines found in the written law and considered that these alone were binding. They refused to believe in angels, spirits, or the resurrection of the body (see Mk 12:18; Acts 23:8), since such tenets were not found in the Law of Moses. They were voluble opponents of the Pharisees, who upheld the oral tradition and the unwritten Torah. At the same time they joined those Pharisees who opposed Jesus, and sided with them in persecuting St. Peter and St. John.

Saints

The holy ones who have led lives of holiness and heroic virtue in union with God by responsiveness to the graces of Christ, the saints enjoy eternal life in heaven. St. Paul often used the term *saints* in a general way as a name for Christians. Feasts of individual saints occur frequently in the liturgy. The feast of All Saints on the first of November commemorates all those uncanonized people who are in heaven. The vast variety of male and female saints from every walk of life witnesses to everyone how powerful God's grace can be and hence inspires all believers that sanctity is possible for them as well. See also **Canonization; Communion of Saints**.

Salvation

The act that saves people from sin and restores them to friendship with God, salvation is God's loving and merciful response to human sinfulness. Derived from a Latin word for "health," the term *salvation* refers to a deed designed to assure spiritual health. It is more than a one-time event in a person's life, since the damage of sin remains and needs to be gradually purified through a lifelong saving process. This is why prayer, fasting, charitable giving, acquisition of virtue, and the graces of the sacraments are vital parts of Christian living and signs of the effective power of salvation.

Salvation History

The interpretation of how God acts in time, salvation history is a vision of history from the viewpoint of God's loving plan to save the world. History is more than a series of facts laid out in sequence. Facts require interpretation and a search for meaning.

Secular versions of history defend various positions, such as the integrity and value of a nation and its origins, heroes, and heroines. In the time of monarchies, histories legitimized kings and queens. With the founding of democracies, new histories illumine this kind of government.

In Scripture, salvation history provides a view of the way in which God has worked in history to save people from sin and bring them to friendship with the divine. Salvation history describes the divine presence working in the lives of patriarchs, kings, prophets, and people of wisdom, shaping them into a covenant community and preparing them for the age of the Messiah. The mighty acts of God in the Old Testament are fulfilled in his mightiest deed, the Incarnation of Jesus Christ.

What Christ did continues in the Church and the sacraments. Chronicled in Scripture and Church history, God's presence and action in history displays a seamless unity from Adam, to Christ, to the present day.

Sanctification

The process of becoming holy by the power of the Spirit, sanctification is a lifelong commitment of the person to be open to the graces of God. It implies a progressive growth in friendship with God and the purification of the soul and body from all sinfulness. Sanctification is an artwork of God. All saints testify that in the final analysis, their holiness is a work of grace.

Sanctification originates in a call from God to embark on the life of holiness. "As he who called you is holy, be holy yourselves in every aspect of your conduct, for it is written, 'Be holy because I am holy'" (1 Pt 1:15-16 NAB; see also Lv 11:45). The call to sanctity is offered to all members of the Church, not just to a favored few. St. Paul makes this clear for the Thessalonians: "This is the will of God, your holiness" (1 Thes 4:3 NAB).

Sanctification best takes place in the context of the community of the Church worshiping, loving, serving, and witnessing. The lives of the saints and the four Gospels are a perennial source of inspiration for the life of holiness.

Sanctifying Grace

Received in baptism and directed to making the person holy, sanctifying grace is a divine gift that endows a person with a stable, supernatural disposition to live in God's presence and act according to God's love (see 2 Cor 5:17-18). It may be thought of as a habit that inclines a person persistently to remain before God and behave out of a motive of divine love.

Sanctity of Life

God is involved with the creation of each human life, thus putting it in a special relationship with Him as its final end. For that reason, human life is sacred. In other words, there is no such thing as a human life that has no fundamental connection with God, who is the Lord of life from its beginning to its end. This is why no one can claim the right to destroy an innocent human being.

Sanctuary

The area where the main altar is situated in a church, the sanctuary is the privileged setting for the celebration of the liturgy of the Eucharist. Besides the altar it contains the lectern for the proclamation of God's Word and the giving of the homily. *The General Instruction of the Roman Missal* indicates that the sanctuary "should be distinguished from the rest of the church by some feature such as a raised floor, special shape, or decoration" (n. 258).

Sanhedrin

Basically the supreme court of the Jews in biblical times, the Sanhedrin in Christ's time had seventy-one members, including priests, elders, and scribes. The Sanhedrin was involved in the trial of Jesus (see Mt 26:59). Though generally opposed to Jesus, the Sanhedrin included men favorable to Christ such as St. Nicodemus and St. Joseph of Arimathea. After the death of Jesus, the Sanhedrin persecuted Christians (see

Acts 4:5-21); was involved in stoning St. Stephen (see Acts 6:12); and harassed St. Paul (Acts 23:15).

Satan
See **Devil; Lucifer.**

Satisfaction for Sin
Though sin is forgiven in the sacrament of reconciliation, there is still need for acts of satisfaction or making amends for sin because the person needs to be purified from any effect of sin that might remain. The confessor gives the penitent a penance as a form of satisfaction by which the penitent makes reparation to God for any offense given. The penitent should unite this act of satisfaction to that of Christ on the cross so that it may derive the value that Christ can give it.

Savior
The name Jesus means "God saves," and he alone is the true Savior of the world.

Scandal
Any attitude or act that leads another to do evil is a scandal. Jesus sternly warned that anyone who would give scandal to children and cause them to sin would be better off having a millstone tied around his neck and being drowned in the sea (see Mt 18:4-6).

Scapular
Based on the Latin for "shoulder," the term *scapular* refers to a garment worn over the shoulders and reaching to the feet. It is commonly worn by members of certain religious orders and symbolizes the voluntary taking on oneself of the yoke and burden of Christ, which is light and sweet (see Mt 11:28-30).

Many of the lay faithful wear an abbreviated form of the scapular consisting of two small pieces of cloth connected by strings and worn over the shoulders. Various religious institutes sponsor the use of such scapulars and have ceremonies of investiture. They impart spiritual benefits for wearing the scapular and the reciting of certain prayers related to Christ, the Virgin Mary, or a saint serving as its patron.

Schism, Eastern
See **Orthodox Church.**

Schism, The Great (or Western)
The lamentable period of forty years (1378–1417) when two and eventually three popes fought each other for control of the Church, the Great (or Western) Schism weakened the Church and set the stage for the Reformation in the following century. To solve the crisis the idea of conciliarism was introduced. It argued that a council should be formed and would have authority over the pope. The Council of

Constance ended the schism in 1417, but the concept of a council governing the Church proved unworkable. The popes regained their authority over the councils and condemned the theory of conciliarism.

Schools, Catholic

With the rise of Western monasticism, especially in the case of the Benedictine Order, the practice of conducting abbey schools began. Eventually this led to the founding of the medieval universities, such as Padua, Paris, Oxford, and Cambridge. To a great extent this education was directed to the formation of monks, clergy, and selected members of the nobility.

During the Counter-Reformation, the Jesuits began opening schools for lay students, training them to be Catholic leaders in society. By the nineteenth century a great number of new religious congregations of men and women were founded specifically to run schools, some primarily for the poor and others for the rising middle classes. The value placed on universal education by the Enlightenment and the needs of science and industry interested the Church, which wanted to make sure that a faith-based education existed alongside state-sponsored schools.

Eventually Catholic school systems sprouted up in Europe and North America. By the late twentieth century, the decline of vocations to religious institutes opened up opportunities for laity to play a major role in the administration and teaching of Catholic school students. State support for Catholic schools exists in most industrialized countries, with the notable exception of the United States, where cultural and political issues militate against it. However, proposals to have some form of state support continue to surface.

Scribes

In ancient cultures, a group of men who had the ability to write were known as scribes. They served as secretaries to rulers and frequently acted as copyists of both legal and religious documents. The Hebrew scribes made copies of Scripture and commentaries on the holy books. Eventually they became teachers and interpreters of Scripture as well.

For a time many of these scribes were priests, but in the New Testament period they were laymen who worked with the priests. They held seats on the Sanhedrin and were linked with the Pharisees opposed to Jesus. However, a few scribes were open to Christ's teachings (see Mt 8:19; Lk 20:39).

Scripture, Sacred

See **Bible**.

Scrupulosity

A constant fear that one has committed a sin when there is no foundation for such a judgment, scrupulosity may result from rigid moral training that overburdens conscience or from some psychological weakness that inclines a person to excessive bouts of an unfounded sense of guilt. Confessors should treat scrupulous people with gentleness and sensitivity and try to reduce their anxiety. In exceptional cases, advice to seek psychological help may be beneficial to the penitent.

Seal of Confession

The priest is bound to keep absolutely secret whatever is heard in the sacrament of confession. This sacred bond between confessor and penitent is known as the seal of confession and admits of no exceptions. What the penitent says to the priest remains "sealed" by the sacrament.

The obligation to preserve confessional confidentiality prevails over any civil legislation that may try to coerce the confessor into revealing what he has heard in confession. A priest who deliberately breaks the confessional seal is automatically excommunicated. Only the Holy See can lift the excommunication.

Second Coming of Christ

Belief in Christ's second coming is affirmed in both the Apostles' and Nicene Creeds. In New Testament times, Christ's return in glory (his *parousia*) was thought to be imminent (see Rv 22:20). As time passed and the Second Coming did not happen, the expectation of an imminent arrival declined and Christ's words about not trying to determine the day or the hour became more important (see Acts 1:7).

Still, throughout Church history an expectation of Christ's imminent coming has experienced a periodic revival. This is especially true in times of crisis or the arrival of a millennium celebration. In the season of Advent especially, the Church emphasizes that we must always be morally and spiritually prepared for Christ's coming, regardless of when the actual moment happens.

Secularism

A perspective on the world that excludes the presence and action of God in creation and history, secularism has become a major influence on contemporary culture. It is preoccupied with a scientific and technological understanding of the world that tends to be rationalistic and leaves little or no room for the knowledge that comes from faith. The result is a reduction of all human effort to a concentration on the world of the here and now, and the rejection of any divine reality or influence on the lives of people or the universe itself.

The Church is responding to secularism with a new evangelization that trusts in the inherent power of the gospel to open hearts to Christ once more. The Church is also reaching out to secular culture to join it in advancing the improvement of human life where possible. It seeks the opportunity for dialogue on the fundamental questions about which thoughtful people have always wondered.

Seminarian

A word based on the Latin for "seed," the term *seminarian* refers to a student for the priesthood. Priestly formation usually requires a college degree with a major in philosophy, followed by four years of theology accompanied by pastoral training in parishes, hospitals, nursing homes, diocesan family apostolates, and other similar apostolic endeavors. Normally a candidate for the seminary must have completed at least two years of college and be spiritually, physically, and psychologically suited for the demands of pastoral ministry. In recent years several seminaries have opened to train second-career or "delayed" vocations to the priesthood.

Sensus Fidei

A supernatural appreciation of the faith by the whole body of the faithful, the *sensus fidei* refers to matters of belief in which all the faithful—bishops, priests, lay faithful, religious—manifest a universal consent on issues of faith and morals. This is possible because all the faithful have been anointed by the Holy Spirit, who teaches and guides them to truth.

Septuagint

An ancient translation of the Hebrew Bible into Greek, the Septuagint was created by Jewish scholars and later adopted by Greek-speaking Christians. The word *Septuagint* comes from the Greek word for "seventy," referring to the seventy Jewish scholars who did the work.

Sermon on the Mount

Christ's most famous sermon, found in St. Matthew chapters five through seven, the Sermon on the Mount begins with the eight beatitudes and is followed by a series of Christ's sayings. Many of these provide a fresh interpretation of the Ten Commandments, with Jesus using the formula, "You have heard it was said ... but I say to you." For example, Jesus cites the sixth commandment that forbids the act of adultery and goes on to teach that even lustful thoughts are also wrong (see Mt 5:27-28).

The sermon fits well with St. Matthew's intention of presenting Jesus as a new Moses. Just as Moses was the first and greatest lawgiver for the Old Covenant, so Jesus is the first and greatest lawgiver for the New Covenant. Moreover, the Ten Commandments were preceded by the covenant union at Sinai, so in St. Matthew the rules of Christ are preceded by the meaning of covenant union as stated in the eight beatitudes. In addition, Christ's two laws of love for God and neighbor are also the covenant foundation for his moral teachings in the Sermon on the Mount.

Finally, Christ's moral teachings drive deeper than the Ten Commandments, since he dwells on attitudes as well as external acts. Jesus is not abrogating the Ten Commandments; rather, he brings out their fuller meaning (see Mt 5:17).

Shepherd, The Good

Biblical culture was largely rural, linked to farms, vineyards, and the raising of cattle and sheep. In a particular way the lives of shepherds attained an idealistic niche in biblical mentality.

The communion of the shepherd with the lambs and sheep was legendary. He knew them by name. They knew his voice and would follow no other. He brought them to still waters, green pastures, defended them against wolves and thieves.

The best-loved king in the Old Testament was the shepherd David, who wrote the Shepherd Psalm (Psalm 23), one of the most beloved prayers in the Bible. Scripture often calls God a shepherd (see Is 40:11; Ez 34:11-16). Jesus called himself the Good Shepherd, listing qualities that a Redeemer should have (see John 10:1-18). Artists have never tired of painting Jesus the Good Shepherd, and for good reason, for it makes him so accessible to us.

In Church life the popes and bishops are seen as shepherds, even carrying a crosier, which is a shepherdlike staff. They are expected to live up to the scriptural ideals of the good shepherd. Even the term *pastoral* so often used for the ministry of priests comes from a shepherd context. The image of the good shepherd evokes attitudes of caring, personal attention, knowledge of people, and even laying down one's life on behalf of the needs of the people.

Shrine

A church or chapel designated as a place of pilgrimage, a shrine honors Christ, Mary, or another saint because of their connection to the sacred place. This may be because the place was the site of a vision of Jesus or Mary, or was the burial place of a saint, or was set apart for some other reason that draws people there for worship, prayer, healing, and growth in faith. Shrines are centers of popular religion. "The religious sense of the Christian people has always found expression in various forms of piety surrounding the Church's sacramental life, such as the veneration of relics, visits to sanctuaries, pilgrimages, processions, the stations of the cross, religious dances, the rosary, medals, etc." (*Catechism*, par. 1674).

Shroud of Turin

The figure of a crucified and scourged man has been impressed on a burial wrapping known as the Shroud of Turin. Many believe that it is the shroud in which Jesus was wrapped during the three days he lay in the tomb. Preserved in the cathedral of Turin, Italy, and exhibited for public viewing, the shroud has been a topic of scholarly debate.

The dating of the shroud changes according to scientific development. For a while scientists concluded it was a medieval artifact. More recent investigations have uncovered tiny remains of plants known to have existed in Palestine at the time of Christ, leading the researchers to believe it does date from the first century. The Church has ruled that the truth about the shroud is not a matter of faith, and Catholics are free to make up their own minds about it.

Sign of the Cross

A gesture that traces the cross of Christ along with words that honor the Trinity, the sign of the cross is made "in the name of the Father and of the Son and of the Holy Spirit." This ritual is used at the beginning of liturgies and acts of devotion.

Signs, Liturgical

Another way of speaking about the numerous rituals that accompany the sacraments is the term liturgical signs. These signs help the participants appreciate the meaning of the liturgies, especially when accompanied by appropriate explanatory prayers. Signs may include kneeling, bowing, standing, or walking in procession, or being anointed with oil, immersed in baptismal water, or blessed with the sign of the cross. The vestments, materials for worship, and elements of a church building are like a living vocabulary silently speaking to the five senses about the transcendent mysteries being celebrated.

Simony

The buying or selling of spiritual things, simony takes its name from the New Testament story of Simon the magician, who wanted to buy spiritual gifts from the apostles (see Acts 8:9-24). Since spiritual gifts belong to God, who shares them freely with us, they are not to be bought and sold.

Sin

An act that breaks down or weakens our relationship with God or harms persons, sin is an offense against God and is contrary to right reason and truth. Sin is any deliberate thought, word, or deed contrary to the eternal law of God. In determining the seriousness of a sin, it is customary to distinguish between mortal and venial sin. See also **Mortal Sin; Sin, Original; Venial Sin.**

Sin, Original

The deprivation of original holiness and justice, original sin is both the act of the first disobedience and its result as described in Genesis chapter three. Since then, all people are born in the state of original sin and need to receive the graces of Christ's redemption through the sacrament of baptism.

Original sin's damage remains even after baptism and is an inner source of moral weakness. However, this weakness is balanced by the gift of being an image of God, which is an inner font of the drive toward God and grace. The *Catechism* (par. 396-421) offers an explanation of the origin and impact of and divine response to original sin. See also **Baptism; Desire, Baptism of; Image of God; Limbo.**

Sistine Chapel

Built by Pope Sixtus IV (1471-84), from whom it gets its name, the Sistine Chapel is the principal chapel of the papal palace and the site of papal elections. It is also particularly famous for the frescoes of Michelangelo, who decorated the ceiling with the story of creation and the entire wall behind the altar with the Last Judgment. In recent times these frescoes were brilliantly restored over a period of fourteen years. This project was funded by Japanese Nippon Television and headed by Fabrizio Manicelli of the Vatican Museum and Gianluigi Colalucci, chief restorer of Vatican art.

Slander

As a lie that harms the reputation of others, slander causes people to make erroneous judgments about them. This is a sin against justice and truth, and repentance from it should include the removal of the harm done to others.

Sloth

Fear of undertaking the labor needed for one's spiritual welfare, sloth is a form of laziness that prevents one from seeking real happiness. Sloth is one of the capital sins. When the demands of loving God and others appear too daunting and the effort seems too difficult, this vice causes a person to be depressed by God's goodness and leads him to abandon the steps required for spiritual and moral living.

Social Justice

From the time that the biblical prophets of Israel preached about justice for the widow, the orphan, and the alien, there has always been a call to people of faith to have a social conscience regarding the needs of the poor and defenseless. With the rise of large cities and the Industrial Revolution in the eighteenth and nineteenth centuries, it became clear that new and virulent forms of social injustice had emerged. From the time of Pope Leo XIII (1878-1903), whose social encyclical *Rerum Novarum* signaled the Church's commitment to social justice in an industrialized world, there has been a consistent and ever-growing body of teaching that calls the Catholic people and all people of good will to bring about justice and peace in the world.

Elements in the teachings about social justice include a belief in the human dignity of every person; the universal destination of the goods of the earth for all people; a just wage; the right to private property; the right to organize to obtain justice; the realization that justice is a condition for peace; and the right of a family to have a decent way of life. The popes have shown major leadership on issues of social justice, and the moral awareness needed for addressing these issues has steadily grown throughout the entire Church.

Sodality

An association of the lay faithful, a sodality is formed both for the faith growth of the members and as a means for charitable endeavors.

Son of God

In a variety of ways the New Testament affirms the divinity of Jesus Christ as Son of God. The great Christological hymns (see Eph 1:3-10; Phil 2:5-11; Col 1:15-20) celebrate the divinity of Christ, as does the first chapter of St. John's Gospel (see Jn 1:1-14). Doubt was cast on Christ's divinity in the fourth century by the African priest Arius. The Council of Nicaea met in 325 to refute Arius and declare anew that Jesus Christ is the only begotten Son of God, of one substance with the Father. The Gospel narratives develop the truth about Christ's divine Sonship (see *Catechism*, par. 441-45).

Son of Man

Jesus used the title *Son of Man* to describe himself. The expression is taken from Daniel 7:13, where the prophet has a vision of a heavenly figure like a "son of man" who comes in the clouds to usher in God's rule. Jesus is related to this image first by bringing

God's kingdom during his earthly ministry and second by his final coming in the *parousia*.

Soul

The spiritual part of a human being, the soul is the center of thinking, loving, judging, and freedom. It is the arena of consciousness. Soul and body together form a unique human being. God immediately creates each individual and immortal soul; it is not "produced" by the parents. At death the body dies, but the soul does not. The soul will be reunited with the body at the resurrection (see *Catechism*, par. 362-68).

Spirit

See **Holy Spirit**.

Spirituality

As another way of speaking about a believer's response to God's call to holiness, the term *spirituality* implies that a person has become more conscious of God's presence and the inner workings of the soul. Throughout Church history various schools of spirituality have arisen that appeal to different types of people. There are particular forms of spirituality associated with the religious orders: Carmelite, Benedictine, Dominican, Franciscan, Jesuit, and others.

In recent times spiritualities suited to the busy lives of contemporary laity have emerged. Spiritualities may include, according to the needs and inclinations of the person, daily devotional prayer, meditation, spiritual reading, the practice of virtues, participation in the Eucharist and the Liturgy of the Hours, the Rosary, acts of charity and service to others, and acts of penance. A spiritual director can be very helpful for anyone pursuing a spiritual life.

Spiritual Works of Mercy

The spiritual works of mercy are these: instruct the ignorant, correct sinners, counsel the doubtful, be patient with sinners and those in error, forgive others, comfort the afflicted, and pray for the living and the dead.

Sponsors for Baptism and Confirmation

Persons who willingly agree to help those about to be baptized or confirmed to follow the demands of the faith, sponsors should be practicing Catholics. They can be very helpful in guiding and encouraging the baptized and confirmed to realize the meaning of these sacraments and the responsibilities incurred.

State of Grace

Believers who are in the state of friendship with God, and have no sins that need to be forgiven, are in the state of grace.

Stations of the Cross

Originating in the Middle Ages and promoted by the Franciscans, the Stations of the Cross is a devotion to the passion of Christ from the moment of his condemnation by Pilate to his burial. Churches place fourteen images, representing scenes from the passion, spaced out on the walls in such a way that a person walks from one to the other until the meditations and prayers are completed. These images range from picturelike representations to abstract artwork. In recent times a fifteenth station recalling Easter is sometimes added so that the full paschal mystery of death and resurrection is considered.

In Lent many parishes have community devotions for the stations. Pope John Paul II has developed an alternative set of stations that broaden the original ones, beginning with the Last Supper and introducing Mary at the cross, where Jesus forms a new Holy Family with St. John and Mary.

Stealing, Theft

Forbidden by the seventh commandment, stealing and theft are wrong because these acts unjustly take and keep someone's property against the will of the owner.

Sterilization

A medical procedure by which a man or a woman becomes unable to beget or conceive children, sterilization undertaken for this purpose is immoral. However, a therapeutic sterilization that is the only means of curing a pathological condition is permissible.

Stewardship

The use of time, talent, and treasure in such a way that God's kingdom on earth is advanced, stewardship has a biblical basis. Jesus praises the wise steward in St. Luke 12:42 and teaches that the "children of light" should be as imaginative in their stewardship as was the clever steward in the parable delivered in St. Luke 16:1-9. The prudent and generous use of one's gifts honors God, enables others to live decent lives, and assists the Church in its mission.

Stigmata

The appearance of all or some of the five wounds of Christ from his passion on the bodies of certain chosen people, the stigmata (plural of the Greek *stigma*, meaning "mark" or "tatoo") are usually associated with saintly and mystical people. Some famous people who received the stigmata are St. Francis of Assisi, St. Catherine of Siena and—in modern times—Blessed Padre Pio.

Stipend

As an offering freely given to a priest for celebrating a Mass for a certain intention, a stipend is today usually termed an offering instead.

Stole

A narrow strip of cloth worn by a priest around his neck and down the front to the knees, the stole follows the liturgical color of the day. Deacons also wear a stole draped over the left shoulder, then across the chest to the right side, where it is fastened.

Subsidiarity

Often mentioned approvingly in the Church's social teaching, subsidiarity is a principle of politics in which the central government acknowledges the freedom and responsibility of competent authorities at local levels. It is a reasonable distribution of power and authority. This supports the theme that higher authorities should not be bothered with doing what lower authorities are capable of handling.

Suicide

The taking of one's own life, suicide is contrary to God's law as enunciated in the fifth commandment. Psychological pressures may diminish the moral culpability of the person committing suicide. The move toward physician-assisted suicide is not morally justified. However, pain killers and palliative care are permissible so long as there is no intention to kill the patient.

Sunday

The Lord's Day, Sunday is the principal day of the week set aside for the Eucharistic celebration. Every Sunday recalls Christ's resurrection and the day that each baptized believer became a new creation in Christ. Because the Sunday Eucharist is the foundation of Christian practice, the faithful are obliged to participate in the Eucharist unless excused for a serious reason.

Supernatural

As that which surpasses natural human understanding and powers, the supernatural comes entirely as a gift of God, as in the case of grace. The very call to eternal life is a supernatural event because it depends on God's free initiative. God alone can give it. These supernatural events surpass the powers of the human mind and will but are given by God out of pure and infinite love.

Superstition

Assigning magical power to certain acts or things, superstition is contrary to trust in God and is opposed to the first commandment.

Surplice

A loose-fitting white garment with sleeves and covering the body from the neck to the knees, the surplice is a choir garb and also is worn by a master of ceremonies at various liturgies.

Symbol

Gestures, words, things, seasons, cosmic imagery, and other forms of symbolic communication are ways in which the invisible realities of God are pointed to especially in celebrating the mysteries of salvation in the liturgy. In the case of the sacraments, which use symbols such as water, bread, and wine, the symbols not only point to, but also contain and produce the realities signified by the power of the Holy Spirit present and active in the sacramental events (see *Catechism*, par. 1145-52).

Synagogue

The meeting place of prayer for the Jewish religion, the synagogue seems to have come into existence when the Jewish people were taken into exile in Babylon and had no temple for worship. By Christ's time and up to the present, synagogues have become regular centers for religious gatherings of Jews. Many synagogues have added a building for Jewish education.

Synod of Bishops; Synod, Diocesan

A meeting in Rome of selected bishops representing the worldwide Church, the Synod of Bishops is an occasion for discussing doctrinal, moral, and pastoral needs of the Church. Since Vatican II the popes have called such synods every few years and published synodal documents that reflect the results of their discussions. A diocesan synod is an assembly of the bishop, priests, and representative lay faithful of a diocese for the purpose of examining the needs of the local Church and offering advice and legislation for the bishop to enact.

Synoptic Gospels

The Gospels of St. Matthew, St. Mark, and St. Luke are called synoptic Gospels because they contain so much similar material in greater or lesser measure and are arranged in a slightly different manner.

Tabernacle

A boxlike receptacle, usually made of precious metal or wood and suitably adorned, the tabernacle is the place where the Blessed Sacrament is reserved. Prior to Vatican II, the tabernacle was placed on the main altar. Now that the altar faces the people, the tabernacle has been relocated to other positions.

Originally, the tabernacle was intended for the reservation of the Eucharist that would be brought to the sick. As faith in the Eucharist deepened, people became aware of the value of silent adoration of the Eucharist. This is why the tabernacle should be located in a prominent place in the church and constructed in such a way that the truth of the real presence of Christ in the Eucharist is manifested (see *Catechism*, par. 1379).

Teaching Office

At the Last Supper, Jesus promised to send the Holy Spirit to abide with the Church and to guide it into truth (see Jn 14:25-26). The gift of the Spirit reposes in the Church's teaching office, which is the Magisterium of the pope and bishops. See also **Magisterium**.

Temperance

One of the cardinal virtues, temperance inclines a person to avoid excess in any endeavor. The temperate person moderates passions, enthusiasms, or any form of extreme behavior without stifling the legitimate fulfillment of plans and purposes that accomplish God's will. Temperance causes balance in the use of material goods and enables the person to keep natural desires within the proper limits.

Temple of Jerusalem

In the earliest days of Jewish religion, the central shrine to God and locus of sacrifice was a simple altar upon which rested the Ark of the Covenant. The space was enclosed by a tent. The tent was replaced when King Solomon built the first temple in Jerusalem around 922 B.C. It was destroyed by the Babylonians in 587 B.C.

To serve the Jewish exiles returning from their Babylonian captivity, a second temple was built by Zerubbabel in 515 B.C. Smaller, modest and far less glorious than Solomon's, this temple was pillaged by various invaders over the centuries. Just before the time of Christ, Herod the Great decided to build a temple whose grandeur would rival that of Solomon's.

The sanctuary was finished in eighteen months in 19 B.C. Then over the next fifty years, the thirty-five acres of temple mount were filled with courtyards, buildings, walls, and powerful stone supports to hold up the extended temple expanse. This was the temple that Jesus knew. It was destroyed by the armies of the Roman general (later emperor) Titus in A.D. 70. See also **Holy of Holies**.

Temptation

The pressure to sin exerted by persons, places, or things, and by the devil's temptation, is experienced in everyday life. The attraction to act against reason and God's commandments can also originate from within one's self. The Gospels report that Jesus experienced temptations, but never sinned.

Resistance to temptation requires vigilance, prayer, self-discipline, acquisition of virtue, and dependence upon God for the graces needed to avoid sin and remain faithful to moral and spiritual principles. For those who give in to temptations to sin, God's mercy is available in the sacrament of reconciliation.

Ten Commandments

The laws by which a person can live the consequences of a covenant with God, the Ten Commandments were given to Moses after the covenant experience at Sinai (see Ex 19:3-6; 20:2-17). The best Christian context for appreciating the Ten Commandments is found in Christ's two commandments of love for God and love for others and self, along with the eight beatitudes. See also **Covenant**.

Testament

The word that characterizes each of the two major divisions of the Bible, testament is another term for covenant. The Old Testament chronicles the covenant relationships between God and people—mainly the Israelites—prior to Christ in forty-six books. The New Testament records the mission and ministry of Jesus Christ, Son of God and Son of Mary, and how the early Church continued the work of Christ's new covenant. This is recorded in twenty-seven books.

Theological Virtues

Assisting Christians to have a prayerful intimacy with the Father, Son, and Spirit, the theological virtues are gifts from God meant to deepen people's loving union with the Trinity. Faith, hope, and love (or charity) are the three theological virtues.

The gift of faith initiates and strengthens a lifelong belief in God and the truths taught by the Church. The gift of hope nurtures the expectation of eternal life and the graces to receive it. The gift of love makes possible the love of God above all else along with love of others and self. These virtues penetrate the moral virtues of prudence, justice, temperance, and fortitude, and foster their growth.

Theology

The art and science of faith seeking understanding, theology reflects on the truths of divine revelation. Theologians seek a deeper understanding of the mysteries of faith to relate them more effectively to people's lives. Theology develops in a special way when truths of divine revelation are denied, misunderstood, or undermined.

In the early Church, for example, the denial of Christ's humanity by the Gnostics and Docetists and the denial of Christ's divinity by the Arians prompted a vigorous theological response. Their defense of the faith produced a greater understanding of these mysteries and created a unique language for communicating the truths that remains helpful to this day.

Theophany

Manifestations of God to people, theophanies are frequently described in Scripture. God appeared to Moses at the burning bush (see Ex 3). When Israel was journeying through the desert, God manifested himself as a pillar of cloud by day and a pillar of fire at night (see Ex 13:21-22). Periodically, God appeared as a radiant cloud over the Ark of the Covenant (see Lv 16:2). While attending the enthronement of a new king at a temple ceremony, Isaiah received a vision of God in glory, during which God called him to be a prophet (see Is 6). Theophanies of God also occurred at the Baptism and transfiguration of Jesus (see Mt 3:16-17; 17:1-8).

Theotokos

The Greek word for "God-bearer," *Theotokos* is a title applied to the Blessed Mother Mary by the Council of Ephesus in 451. The Council made this pronouncement in response to a false teaching that said Mary was only the mother of the human Jesus, not the Jesus who was also Son of God. A prayerful outcome of this council was the creation of the second part of the Hail Mary, which begins with the words, "Holy Mary, Mother of God, pray for us ..."

Tithe

A tenth of one's income or possessions given to God, a tithe is usually a donation of a tenth of one's income to the parish or other works of religion. Its biblical origin may be found in Leviticus 27:30. The most extensive section of Scripture devoted to charitable giving is in chapters eight, nine, and eleven of 2 Corinthians.

St. Paul urges generosity when he writes, "Consider this: Whoever sows sparingly will also reap sparingly, and whoever sows bountifully will also reap bountifully. Each must do as already determined, without sadness or compulsion, for God loves a cheerful giver" (2 Cor 9:6-7 NAB).

Titular Bishop

All bishops must have a title that describes their pastoral responsibility, such as the name of the diocese that they shepherd. However, bishops who have not yet been named head of a diocese are granted titular or "titled" status of a diocese that no longer exists due to demographic changes, historical shifts, military conquests by members of other religions or ideologies, or some other reason.

Torah

Strictly speaking, the Torah refers to the first five books of Scripture. Meaning both "instruction" and "law," the Torah has also been more broadly applied to the whole Old Testament and even to the entire body of Jewish religious literature derived in Bible times from priests, prophets, and sages.

Tradition

The living transmission of the gospel preached and witnessed to by Christ, tradition passes on in its entirety the Word of God entrusted to the apostles by Christ and the Holy Spirit. The oral preaching of the apostles and the written message of salvation conserved in Scripture are handed on as the deposit of faith through apostolic succession in the Church. Tradition and Scripture flow from a single source of revelation of God in Jesus Christ.

The Church does not derive certainty about revealed truths from Scripture alone, but from both Scripture and Tradition. Theological, liturgical, disciplinary, and devotional traditions of local churches contain and yet are distinguished from Apostolic Tradition (see *Catechism,* par. 83).

Transcendence

The majesty and mystery of God are realities ultimately beyond full human understanding. These realities are God's transcendence. At the same time, God unveils his mystery to people and gives them the capacity to have a progressive experience and understanding of the divine, though this is never complete.

God has planted in each person an unquenchable desire to know and love the Lord. Through creation, the reflection on the human person, and direct revelation, God responds to the hunger he has planted in the human heart (see *Catechism,* par. 31-35; 50). The greatest revelation took place in Jesus Christ, who is our immediate access to the reality and wonder of God.

Transfiguration

A mysterious episode on a high mountain where Jesus appears in glory to St. Peter, St. James, and St. John, the Transfiguration confirms St. Peter's confession of faith in Christ and also emphasizes that Jesus will have to suffer before entering his glory (see Mt 17: 1-8; Mk 9:2-8; Lk 9:28-36). As at the Baptism of Jesus, so now again the Father is heard saying that Jesus is his beloved Son. The Transfiguration was meant to strengthen the faith of the disciples when faced with the passion of Christ. It also reminded them that they also would have to face the cross as part of their commitment to Christ and the gospel.

Transubstantiation

Adapted from the scholastic philosophy of the Middle Ages, the term transubstantiation was used to describe the change of the substance of bread into the substance of the Body of Christ and the change of the substance of wine into the substance of the Blood of Jesus at the consecration of the bread and wine at Mass. Though the substances are entirely changed, the species, or appearances of bread and wine, remain the same. This miracle is brought about by the power of the Holy Spirit through the ministry and words of an ordained priest or bishop.

Trent, Council of

Called by Pope Paul III, the Council of Trent convened twenty-five times from 1545 to 1563. At this ecumenical council the bishops responded to the challenges of the Protestant Reformation and instituted needed reforms, such as a renewal of the liturgy, the establishment of seminaries, and the requirement that bishops live in their dioceses. The doctrinal teachings of the council dwelt on Scripture and tradition, faith and good works, grace and justification, and the role and meaning of the seven sacraments. There was a special emphasis on the Eucharist and the ordained priesthood.

It was hoped that clarification of these doctrinal issues could be a source of reunion of Catholics and Protestants, but this did not happen. Nevertheless, the influence of the Council of Trent was enormous and productive, unleashing tremendous energies of faith and practice that had an impact right up to modern times.

Triduum

Three days of liturgical or devotional prayer, a triduum is best exemplified by Holy Thursday, Good Friday, and the Easter Vigil, which is known as the Easter Triduum. There are also triduums for feasts of Mary and the other saints according to local customs.

Trinity

The mystery of one God in three
Persons, the Trinity is the central truth
of Christian religion and the root of the
Church's faith as expressed in the creed.
The truth of the Trinity could not be
known by the human mind unless it
had been revealed—as it was by Jesus
Christ—and the gift of faith was given
in order to know it.

Typology

The recognition of persons, places, or
things in the Old Testament as types to
be fulfilled in Christ, typology is the
process by which such a discernment
occurs. For example, the sacrifice of the
Passover lamb was a type of the sacrifice
of Christ. Typology demonstrates the
unity of God's plan of salvation seen in
Scripture.

Ultramontanism

Named from the Latin phrase meaning "beyond the mountains," Ultramontanism describes groups of European Catholics who lived north of the Alps and gave pronounced support to the pope when other Catholics were seeking maximum independence from papal authority. Originating in the seventeenth century, Ultramontanism was a pro-papal response to French Gallicanism—and similar movements in other Catholic countries—that sought to establish a national church freed from papal authority. Ultramontanists considered national churches a threat to Catholic unity.

The dogma of papal infallibility, proclaimed at Vatican I, was partially an effect of the Ultramontanist movement, which succeeded in reinforcing papal authority. The teachings about the collegiality of pope and bishops at Vatican II addressed related, complementary issues that could not be taken up at Vatican I because of its sudden termination as a result of the Franco-Prussian War.

Unction

Referring to an anointing with oil, the term *unction* was formerly associated with the sacrament of extreme unction or final anointing. The sacrament has been renamed the sacrament of anointing, which may be given to those who are gravely ill, to those about to have a serious operation, or to those about to die. Unction, or anointing with oil, is also given at baptism, confirmation, and holy orders.

Uniate Churches

Ever since the Eastern Schism in 1054, there have been periodic attempts to reunite the Eastern and Western Churches. A number of Eastern Christians have entered into communion with Rome, and they recognize the authority of the pope. They have retained their own rites, liturgical languages, and canon law.

The Orthodox Churches called these Christians uniates after the treaty of Brest-Litovsk in 1595. It was meant to be a demeaning term, implying that these believers had given up their culture, liturgy, and religious identity by joining Rome. But members of the Eastern Catholic Churches reject the title uniate, pointing out that their communities are flourishing and their liturgies are genuinely Eastern, especially due to the encouragement given by Vatican II's "Decree on the Eastern Catholic Churches."

Unity, Christian
See Ecumenism.

Urbi et Orbi
In Latin, "for the city and the world," *urbi et orbi* is the name for a blessing given by the pope to the city of Rome and to the whole world. The pope gives such a blessing from the balcony in front of St. Peter's basilica on Christmas and Easter. Popes also give this blessing at the time of their election, and from the balconies of the other three Roman basilicas (St. John Lateran, St. Mary Major, St. Paul Outside the Walls) on special occasions.

Usury
The taking of excessive and unjust interest on a loan, usury is a sin against justice and charity. Originally, Jewish and Christian tradition applied the term usury to taking any kind of interest on a loan. Eventually, in the eighteenth century, the Church recognized the legitimacy of asking for fair interest on a loan.

Ut Unum Sint
An encyclical by Pope John Paul II on the role of the papacy and the difficulties this presents for ecumenism, *Ut Unum Sint* (*That They All May Be One*) maintains the authority of the pope but also asks Church leaders and their theologians to engage in a patient and fraternal dialogue about the issue. Reminding everyone that in the first Christian millennium the primacy of the bishop of Rome was accepted, John Paul II asks that a way may be found to restore this agreement in the third millennium. He pays special attention to the Orthodox Church, with whom Catholicism has an intimate connection on matters such as the doctrine of the Eucharist and the priesthood, the celebration of the Christian mysteries, and an authentic episcopate. The encyclical appeals for renewed ecumenical dialogue.

Vatican City

A 108-acre enclave, Vatican City is an independent state, the last of the Papal States and recognized as a national entity since the signing of the Lateran Treaty with Italy in 1929. It has been the residence of the popes since the end of the Avignon papacy in 1377. Over the centuries the popes added many of the present buildings. Today most of the administrative offices of the Church (the Curia) are housed there. Its centerpiece is St. Peter's Basilica, which serves as an imposing symbol of the universal Church, along with the residence of the pope, who rules the Church, in collegial unity with the world's bishops, from the Vatican.

Vatican Council I

The twentieth ecumenical council, convened by Pope Pius IX in 1870, the first Vatican Council addressed issues such as the infallibility of the pope and the power of reason to know the existence of God. The council fathers taught that God's existence could be known by reason's reflections on the visible works of creation that point to an invisible Creator. However, since reason acts with a nature darkened by original sin, it is not always easy for reason to know God. Hence, revelation in Tradition and Scripture is a more certain way of coming to know God through faith.

The council fathers also declared the doctrine of the infallibility of the pope on matters of faith and morals. The role of the bishops and the whole body of the faithful was not addressed at this council since its proceedings were interrupted by the Franco-Prussian war. Vatican II's doctrine on the collegiality of bishops in union with the pope, and on the inability of the whole body of the faithful to err on matters of faith and morals because of the gifts of the Holy Spirit to the Church, complemented and rounded out the initiatives of Vatican I on this matter. See **Infallibility;** *Sensus Fidei.*

Vatican Council II

Called into session by Pope John XXIII, the twenty-first ecumenical council was convened as Vatican Council II on October 11, 1962. Council sessions were held each year from 1962 through 1965, always in the autumn.

Prior councils were called to respond to challenges to right doctrine and major crises affecting the Church. The unique feature of Vatican II was the absence of these types of concerns.

Instead, the council fathers turned their attention to the pastoral needs of the Church in a world undergoing profound changes due to industrialization, technology, and the communications revolution. Serious attention was given to the renewal of the liturgy, the meaning of the Church, religious liberty, ecumenism, interfaith relations, and dialogue with all people of good will. The bishops dealt with the needs of the laity, clergy, religious, and Catholic education.

In a remarkable series of documents, the bishops provided the universal Church with a pastoral vision that was positive, Spirit-filled, and evangelizing. The interpretation of the council did lead to contrary conclusions, but gradually, under the leadership of Pope John Paul II—whose lengthy reign has given him the time to assist the Church to see the authentic meaning of the council—its real meaning is beginning to take hold. Efforts to disengage it from previous councils and tradition have not succeeded. By all accounts it was the greatest religious event of the twentieth century, and its impact will be felt for many years to come.

Veneration of the Saints

From the very beginning of the Church, veneration, respect, and devotion was given to Mary, the apostles, and the first martyrs, all of whom had known Jesus and faithfully witnessed to him. As Church history progressed, the veneration of saints continued by honoring men and women who led lives of prayer and self-denial as witnesses to Christ. Their heroic virtues were publicly recognized in their canonization as saints.

This veneration also extends to the relics of these saints and to objects and images associated with them. It is essential to distinguish the act of veneration from adoration and worship, which belong to God alone.

Venial Sin

An act that fails to adhere to God's law but does not destroy divine life in the soul, venial sin diminishes and weakens the soul's capacity for virtuous acts. "One commits venial sin, when in a less serious matter, he does not observe the standard prescribed by the moral law, or when he disobeys the moral law in a grave matter, but without full knowledge or without complete consent" (*Catechism,* par. 1862).

Veritatis Splendor

Taking a unique approach for an encyclical on Christian morality, Pope John Paul II's *Veritatis Splendor* (*The Splendor of Truth*) outlines the principles of morality as well as addressing certain erroneous moral theories. John Paul bases Christian morality on the truth, beauty, and goodness of God. The truth of God attracts the longing of the mind for certainty. The goodness and beauty of God appeal to the human heart that yearns for happiness.

The encyclical begins with a meditation on the story of the rich young man who comes to Christ asking what he must do to obtain eternal life (see Mt 19:16-26). The pope notes that Christ's reply tells us that goodness requires contact with God, the source of goodness; that morality includes obedience to God's commandments; and finally, that holding fast as a disciple to the person of Christ is essential for obtaining the strength to be moral. The three goals of this encyclical are (1) to reflect on the entirety of the Church's moral teachings; (2) to show people the splendor of truth that is Christ himself; (3) to figure out what interpretations of Christian morality are not consistent with the gospel and to contrast these with authentic teaching.

Vespers

Another name for Evening Prayer in the Liturgy of the Hours, Vespers constitutes, along with Morning Prayer, one of the hinges of the daily official prayer of the Church.

Vestments

The robes worn by bishops, priests, deacons, and acolytes for liturgical services, formal vestments have been prescribed for worship since the fourth century, when house liturgies were moved to church settings.

Viaticum

The Holy Eucharist given to dying persons is called viaticum, a Latin word that means "to journey with." It assures the persons that the Real Presence of Jesus Christ is with them in the passage from this world to eternal life.

Vicar

A vicar is someone who acts in the place of another. Dioceses have vicar-generals, clerics who act in the name of the residential bishop and carry out his wishes. Parishes have parochial vicars, priests who assist the pastor and represent him in his absence.

Vicar of Christ

A title most often applied to the pope, Vicar of Christ formally became a papal title in the reign of Eugene III (1145–53). Vatican II says that bishops also are vicars of Christ (*Lumen Gentium*, 27).

Vice

The opposite of virtue, vice is an ingrained habit acquired by repeated sin. A vice violates the norms of morality. The vices are usually identified with the seven capital sins. Confession and repentance restore the soul to grace, but a concerted effort, aided by grace, is needed to reverse the self-destructive habit until its opposite virtue replaces it.

Vigil

In Catholic usage the term *vigil* refers to liturgies on the evening before great feasts, most evidently the Easter Vigil on Holy Saturday night. In earlier times, a vigil could last the entire night with periodic times set aside for psalms, hymns, and readings from Scripture and other sacred writings. Today, Saturday evening liturgies are often called vigil Masses.

Vigil Light

Candles burned before shrines of Christ, Mary, and the other saints, vigil lights are symbols of prayer that people light for various intentions. The candle, which may burn for a few hours or a full week, "stands watch" in place of the person who cannot always be there, serving as a symbol of the prayer the person wishes to offer.

Virgin Birth of Christ

The doctrine that Jesus was virginally conceived and virginally born, the Virgin Birth of Christ is attested to by the conversation Mary had with the angel Gabriel at the Annunciation. Gabriel appears to Mary and announces that she will be the mother of a male child, whom she will call Jesus. "He will be great, and will be called the Son of the Most High" (see Lk 1:32).

Mary wonders how this could happen since she is not married yet and has not had relations with her designated husband. Gabriel tells her this will be a conception caused directly by God. "The Holy Spirit will come upon you, and the power of the Most High will overshadow you; therefore the Child to be born will be called holy, the Son of God" (Lk 1:35) The Church confesses in her creeds that Jesus Christ was conceived and born of the Virgin Mary by the power of the Holy Spirit without any intervention of human seed (see *Catechism*, par. 496).

Virgin Mary, The

The Church teaches that Mary was always a virgin, before, during, and after the birth of Jesus. Some claim the Gospels imply that Mary had other children. St. Luke writes that Mary gave birth to her firstborn son (2:7). Does this mean she had other offspring? No. The expression "firstborn" was a legal one and did not assume the begetting of other children.

St. Matthew reports that St. Joseph had no relations with Mary "until" she bore a son (1:25). But in the original language, this way of speaking makes no judgment about the future, unlike this use of such language today.

The Gospels speak of the "brothers

and sisters" of Jesus as in St. Mark 6:3. But their absence when the boy Jesus was found in the temple seems to indicate there were no other children. At the cross, would not Jesus have entrusted Mary to a brother or sister instead of to St. John?

Finally, the historical belief in Mary's perpetual virginity was not contested when the memory of the phrase "brothers and sisters of Jesus" was very much alive. The Eastern Church concludes that the brothers and sisters of Jesus were the children of St. Joseph by his first marriage. The Western Church, following St. Jerome, believes they were cousins, especially since the word in the original language meant both sibling and cousin.

Mary's perpetual virginity flows from her being the mother of the Son of God and her total and undivided heart's dedication to God.

Virtue

An ingrained habit and attitude that inclines one toward good acts, a virtue is an essential building block of the moral life. The moral virtues of prudence, justice, temperance, and fortitude are acquired by human effort aided by grace. They are obtained by hearing inspiring stories about the practice of virtue and also by experiencing the living witness of these virtues by one's family and friends and public role models.

The virtues are gained as well by repeated acts of a given virtue until it is engraved into the soul and behavior of the person. Finally, the moral virtues grow through the power of grace and the formative influence of the theological virtues of faith, hope, and love (or charity), which are direct gifts from the Holy Spirit.

Virtues, Theological

Given by the Holy Spirit, the theological virtues of faith, hope, and love (or charity) enable a person to respond willingly to God's call and will and so become ready for eternal life. Faith makes it possible for persons to respond to God's self-revelation with belief, commitment, and the desire to share this gift with others. Hope opens the person to desire eternal life and to await it with firm trust, along with the graces to receive it. Love (or charity) moves people to love God above all else and their neighbors as themselves because of love of God.

Charity is the soul of all virtues: "It articulates and orders them among themselves; it is the source and the goal of their Christian practice. Charity upholds and purifies our human ability to love, and raises it to the supernatural perfection of divine love" (*Catechism*, par. 1827).

Vision, Beatific

See **Beatific Vision**.

Visions

Scripture reports numerous occasions of visions of God, angels, and holy people. Moses has a vision of God at the burning bush (see Ex chapter 3). Isaiah beheld an appearance of God at the temple (see Is chapter 6). An angel appeared to Mary (see Lk chapter 1). Moses and Elijah were part of the vision of the Transfiguration (see Lk 9:30) seen by St. Peter, St. James, and St. John. The book of Revelation is packed with visions seen by its author, St. John.

Church history is filled with reports of visions right up to the present day. When the visionary receives "private revelations," these are tested seriously by the Church as to their authenticity. Such revelations do not add anything to the definitive revelation given by Christ, but they may help people live the faith more fully. Christians may not accept revelations that claim to surpass or correct divine revelation given in Christ and fulfilled by him.

Visitation of Mary

At the Annunciation the angel Gabriel told Mary that her aged cousin, St. Elizabeth, had conceived a son and was then in her sixth month of pregnancy. Mary went to visit Elizabeth and help her with the forthcoming birth. The opening scene of her visitation occasioned the quickening of the baby in Elizabeth's womb and a God-given insight to her about Mary's gift.

St. Elizabeth praises Mary for having believed what the angel told her and declares that Mary is most blessed among women and that her womb is blessed (see Lk 1:42). Mary responds with the canticle called the *Magnificat,* a soaring hymn of praise that is now sung every night at Evening Prayer in the Liturgy of the Hours all over the world.

Vocation

Based on the Latin word for "calling," vocation describes the many ways that God calls every human being. In his creation of each human soul, God plants the call to know, love, and serve him so as to achieve eternal happiness in heaven. Scripture notes that God calls all people to a life of holiness (see Lv 11:44-45). Jesus repeats this call by saying that people should be perfect and merciful as God is (see Mt 5:48; Lk 6:36).

God calls the lay faithful to bring God's kingdom to the world by engaging in temporal affairs and by witnessing to and applying the principles and practices of the Gospel (see *Catechism,* par. 898). In a special way, the word vocation has been applied to the call God gives to certain people to join religious life or the priesthood.

Votive Mass

Besides the regular Sunday and daily Masses, there are votive Masses of the mysteries of Christ, or in honor of Mary or another saint, which are options provided for the devotion of the people.

Vow

A formal and free promise made to God in the presence of the Church, a vow is usually associated with commitment to the consecrated life and the practice of the evangelical counsels of poverty, chastity, and obedience. Members of religious institutes normally take first vows after the completion of a novitiate and final vows several years later. The taking of vows asserts that one will be committed to witnessing Christ's kingdom both in heaven and on earth and dedicated to embodying a good that must be fulfilled by the virtue of religion.

Vulgate

St. Jerome's translation of the Bible from Hebrew and Greek into Latin, the Vulgate is so called because that was the language of ordinary people, in contrast to the upper classes who still spoke Greek. Latin was considered the language of the masses, the *vulgus* or vulgar way of talking. Because of archaeological discoveries of ancient libraries and languages in the last 150 years, there have been a number of new translations of Scripture that reflect a burgeoning linguistic scholarship.

Wage, Just

Another name for a living wage, a just wage is a fair salary that results from an agreement between an employer and employee in which each agrees to the terms of the employment. A just wage is deemed sufficient to support the employee and his family. It should also be large enough to allow the worker to prepare for old age and periods of unemployment.

Papal encyclicals have dealt with the question of a proper wage relative to changing times and needs. Blessed Pope John XXIII wrote in *Mater et Magistra* that "workers should be paid a wage that allows them to live a truly human life." Pope John Paul II addressed this issue in *Laborem Exercens*, noting that "just remuneration for the work of an adult who is responsible for a family means remuneration which will suffice for establishing and properly maintaining a family and providing security for its future."

In modern societies there are also social benefits provided by governments to supplement financial compensation. However, in consumerist cultures the desire for material goods as well as what constitutes family needs has led to both parents working to keep up with these expectations. This is a development whose effect on the health of families has attracted the concern both of social observers and religious leaders.

War, Morality of

See **Just War Theory.**

Water

Frequently used in Church services, water is the central element in the sacrament of baptism where the candidate is either immersed in water or has water poured on the head, in each instance three times. The priest accompanies the water ceremony with the words, "I baptize you in the name of the Father and of the Son and of the Holy Spirit."

At Mass the priest adds a few drops of water to the wine with the prayer, "By the mystery of this water and wine may we come to share in the divinity of Christ, who humbled himself to share in our humanity." The Church also, by means of a blessing, makes Holy Water, which is used for a variety of blessings.

Scripture cites numerous instances of the use of water for practical as well as ritual purposes. The fourth chapter of St. John's Gospel describes Jesus encountering a Samaritan woman at Jacob's well, where a dialogue emerges in which water's value as satisfying physical thirst becomes the image of Christ's mission to minister to spiritual thirst.

Western Schism
See **Schism, The Great (or Western).**

Will of God
In the Our Father one of the petitions states, "Thy will be done." When Jesus experienced his agony in the Garden of Gethsemane, he prayed that the cup of suffering might pass from him, only to say immediately afterward that the Father's will should be done, and not his own. Throughout all Scripture the theme of submitting to the Father's will is constant. Because the Father is so loving, he only wills what is fulfilling and hopeful for all people; hence the search for God's will through prayer and discernment is essential.

The two most consequential surrenders to the Father's will were performed by God's Son and Mary. The Son spoke to the Father, "Then I said, 'As is written of me in the scroll, Behold, I come to do your will, O God'" (Heb 10:7 NAB). Mary echoes this submission when she says to the angel Gabriel, "Behold, I am the handmaid of the Lord. May it be done to me according to your word" (Lk 1:38 NAB). Those two responses to God's will brought about the beginning of the salvation of the world. All authentic spirituality brings people to see the desirability of knowing God's will and acting on it.

Wine
The climate and soil of the Holy Land has been favorable to the growth of grapes and the making of wine since biblical times. Scripture makes numerous references to vines, vineyards, and wine as symbols of the relationship of people to God and finally to the Eucharist itself.

Isaiah's "Song of the Vineyard" describes God as planting vines, nurturing them, and then looking for juicy grapes, only to find wild ones of little use. Who is this vine? "The vineyard of the Lord of hosts is the house of Israel" (Is 5:7). The prophet proceeds to pronounce judgment on those who fail to do God's will.

Jesus speaks in a similar vein about what happens to the branches that do not stay fastened to him, the true vine. "Anyone who does not remain in me will be thrown out like a branch and wither; people will gather them and throw them into a fire and they will be burned" (Jn 15:6 NAB). On a more positive note, Jesus' miracle turning water into wine at Cana becomes a symbolic forecast of the wine that will be changed into his Blood in the Eucharist.

At Pentecost St. Peter, in the first Christian sermon, describes the power of the Holy Spirit and the manifestation of the Church to be like barrels of fresh wine predicted by Joel: "On that day the mountains shall drip new wine" (Jl 4:18 NAB).

Wisdom

When the people of Israel were brought to Babylon and later given contact with Greek and Roman culture, they were introduced to the wisdom teachings of those peoples. Spirit-inspired writers purified and incorporated this wisdom into the covenant traditions of their people. Eventually, guided by the Spirit, these wisdom writings became part of Scripture in the section known as the wisdom books.

Among other things, these books are a reminder that knowledge alone is not enough; wisdom, which senses the ultimate meaning of life from the viewpoint of God and eternal destiny, provides an incomparable guide to everyday life. The first chapter of St. John's Gospel, which speaks of Christ as an incarnate *Logos* or Word, draws its inspiration from the wisdom books and presents a Jesus who is living wisdom.

Every Christian has available the greatest of the Spirit's seven gifts, that of wisdom. Knowledge discloses what is. Wisdom reveals what should be.

Witness

It is one thing to hear and speak God's Word; it is another thing to practice it. That is what witness is all about.

Pope Paul VI wrote about witness in his apostolic letter *Evangelii Nuntiandi* (*On Evangelization*): "Modern man listens more willingly to witnesses than to teachers, and if he does listen to teachers, it is because they are witnesses.... It is therefore primarily by her conduct and by her life that the Church will evangelize the world, in other words, by her living witness of fidelity to the Lord Jesus—the witness of poverty and detachment, of freedom in the face of the powers of this world, in short, the witness of sanctity" (41). The ultimate form of this witness is blood martyrdom; in fact, the term *martyrdom* actually means "witness."

Just before his ascension Jesus commissioned his apostles to evangelize the world and said to them, "You will be my witnesses in Jerusalem, throughout Judea and Samaria, and to the ends of the earth" (Acts 1:8 NAB). The credibility of the Christian message is vastly increased by a persuasive witness that shows people how and why salvation is necessary and has been the source of peace and joy to millions for two thousand years.

Woman

In God's plan for the world he created man and woman. They were created in God's image for one another and meant to complement each other. Christ has redeemed man and woman precisely as male and female.

Mary's "yes" brought a human being, a woman, into a union with God that surpasses all human expectation. Mary witnesses to the truth that the essence of human dignity lies in radical self-giving, not in self-assertion or domination. While it is true that male domination, sometimes abusive, is transmitted by culture, the real source of this tendency is sin.

The liberation of women from patterns of domination should be a freedom *for*, not a freedom *against*. Women's freedom is part of the vocation of both men and women that preserves their originality and destiny. Originally there was equality in their diversity. This equality must be recovered.

Pope John Paul II asserts that the Christian gospel is a consistent protest against whatever offends against the true dignity of women. Christ's preaching about self-giving love was appreciated by women, and that is why they were faithful to him during his ministry and at Calvary when all the males, save John, had fled. John Paul draws attention to the canticle of love in 1 Corinthians 13:1-13 and suggests that this love is characteristic of the feminine genius in the Church. For further study, see the Holy Father's encyclical *Mulieris Dignitatem* (*Dignity of Women*).

Women's Ordination

The question of whether women can be ordained priests has been debated in the Catholic Church since the mid-1970s. The matter was influenced by modern feminist theory, theological speculations about the nature of the priesthood, and the decision of the Anglican Communion to accept women as priests. Pope Paul VI responded to this issue in his declaration *Inter Insigniores* (*Among the Characteristics*).

This declaration's key teaching is as follows: "The Sacred Congregation for the Doctrine of the Faith judges it necessary to recall that the Church, in fidelity to the example of the Lord, does not consider herself authorized to admit women to priestly ordination." It was noted that Christ, who in other respects was countercultural regarding women of his time, did not call women to be among the twelve. The apostles continued this practice.

Pope Paul further commented on the significance of Christ's manhood for those who stand in his place as priests. Those who act in the Church *in persona Christi* must be able to represent

Christ as the Bridegroom and Head of the Church. Pope John Paul II reiterated the main points of this teaching in his statement *Ordinatio Sacerdotalis* (*Priestly Ordination*).

Word of God

The full content of revelation as expressed in the Holy Bible, the Word of God is proclaimed in the Church to call people to faith and open them to the transforming power of the Spirit. The first chapter of St. John's Gospel also speaks of God's Word (or *Logos*) as the only begotten Son of God who is the fullness of God's revelation. This Word took flesh and became the incarnate Word, true God and true man for our salvation.

Work

Bodily or mental effort undertaken for a given purpose, work was originally part of life in the garden of paradise according to the Genesis narrative. God told Adam to take care of the garden and nurture it (see Gn 2:15). Work is essential to human improvement and dignity. It is a means to both material and spiritual progress.

The Church teaches that work is basically honorable; reminds us that Jesus was a carpenter for most of his life; and has made St. Joseph the patron of workers. The Church's social doctrine addresses the social, economic, and political problems that workers face due to scientific progress and seeks a humane response prompted by the teachings of Scripture and Tradition.

World

Variously called creation, earth, or universe, the world encompasses all that is and owes its existence to God's creating intention and power. Scripture teaches that God called the works of creation "good," and made man and woman in "his own image and likeness" (see Gn 1:27, 31).

In the New Testament the term *world* sometimes has a negative meaning, pointing to the forces that opposed the work of Jesus and the Holy Spirit (see, for example, 1 Jn 2:15-17). It is in this sense that Jesus says he has come to redeem the world from sin. The world will achieve its goal and fulfillment when it is changed into the "new heavens and new earth" in the fullness of God's kingdom (see *Catechism,* par. 1042-50).

Worship

The first act of the virtue of religion is worship, which calls people to adore and honor God. The celebration of the Christian sacraments in the liturgy is the Church's principal form of worship, especially in the Eucharist, the summit and source of the Christian life.

Wreath, Advent

A popular custom in most churches, the
Advent wreath is a circle of evergreen
boughs, adorned with four candles,
each one designed to mark the passing
of one of the four weeks of Advent.
Usually three of the candles are purple,
reflecting the color of the vestments in
Advent. The other candle is rose-
colored for the third Sunday: *Gaudete*
(or Rejoice) Sunday. The wreath is
sometimes suspended from the ceiling,
but more commonly it is placed on a
stand in the sanctuary.

Xavier, Francis

Born in Spain in 1506, St. Francis Xavier entered the University of Paris at age eighteen, where he met St. Ignatius Loyola, who was forming the beginning of the Jesuit Order. St. Francis became one of the original seven members who took vows in 1534 and were ordained three years later. In 1541 he sailed for Asia as a missionary.

St. Francis brought the faith to Goa, Malacca, Japan, and China, and converted approximately thirty thousand people to Catholicism. He died of exhaustion and fever on the island of Shangchwan, near the Chinese port of Canton, in 1552. In terms of missionary zeal, St. Francis Xavier has been compared to St. Paul.

One account of his efforts states that he baptized such a large number of people on a given day that he was so wearied he could scarcely raise his arm. In one of his letters, thinking of the shortage of missionaries, he wrote that he thought of going around to the universities of Europe and crying out like a madman to get the attention of the intellectuals who seemed to prize learning more than sharing the faith and converting souls. He would say to them, "What a tragedy: How many souls are being shut out of heaven and falling into hell, thanks to you."

St. Francis was canonized in 1662 and made patron of the missions in 1927. Many parishes today have a "novena of grace" seeking his intercession from March 4 through March 12.

Y

Yahweh (YHWH)

The Hebrew name for God that Moses received on Mount Horeb at the scene of the burning bush, Yahweh (YHWH) means, "I AM" or "HE IS," and expresses the essential personal existence of God (see Ex 3:13-15). Scholars call the name Yahweh a "tetragrammaton" because of the four consonants Y, H, W, H—the way it is written in the Hebrew text.

As an act of reverence, as well as a fear that God's name would be misused, the Jews did not utter the name Yahweh, but rather substituted the term *Adonai,* a word that means "my Lord." Only a high priest might pronounce the name Yahweh, once a year, when he entered the Holy of Holies of the temple on the Day of Atonement to offer a sacrifice. In the New Testament Jesus is frequently designated as *kyrios,* the Greek word used in the Septuagint to translate Yahweh. This use of *kyrios* basically affirmed Christ's divinity, since the name Yahweh had been strictly reserved for God.

Zeal, Religious

Enthusiastic behavior in the cause of
the faith, religious zeal works best when
it is motivated by love and moderated
by prudence and temperance. Religious
moralists, when they go overboard, will
tend toward legalistic casuistry—a zeal
that prefers rules to people. On the
other hand, people who take religion so
casually that they verge on the edge of
indifference are so lacking in zeal that
they cannot summon up even minimal
energy on behalf of the faith.

Jesus modeled the best approach to
religious zeal. His preaching and behavior were such models of fidelity to the
Law, while at the same time solicitous
of human dignity, that the legalistic religious leaders disliked him and thought
he was undermining the faith. But
when he cleansed the temple of those
very same religious leaders for commer-
cializing unfairly and shamelessly the
cost of sacrificial offerings and the
exchange of money, he demonstrated
an aspect of zeal that required moral
courage and enthusiasm for God's
house. As he said, "My house shall be a
house of prayer, but you have made it a
den of thieves" (Lk 19:46 NAB).